# Energy I

## 5th edition

### By Eric and Katrina Rasbold

2nd edition 2013

3rd edition 2014

4th edition 2016

5th edition 2018

ISBN-13: 978-1492769453

ISBN-10: 1492769452

Text Copyright © 2018 Eric and Katrina Rasbold All Rights Reserved

# Table of Contents

Chapter 1 - What is Energy Magic?..................................................................................1
Chapter 2 - Tenets and Terminology of Energy Magic .....................................................5
Chapter 3 - The "Universal" of Bio-Universal ...................................................................9
Chapter 4 - The "Bio" of Bio-Universal ............................................................................13
Chapter 5 - About Energy ................................................................................................20
Chapter 6 - The Power of Intention .................................................................................21
Chapter 7 - Properties of Energy – What Speeds It Up?................................................25
Chapter 8 - Properties of Energy – What Slows It Down? .............................................41
Chapter 9 - Properties of Energy – In Summation .........................................................58
Chapter 10 - Bringing It All Together ..............................................................................59
Chapter 11 - Take Back Your Power Eggs .....................................................................61
Chapter 12 - The River Meditation .................................................................................63
Chapter 13 - Pray and/or Meditate ..................................................................................65
Chapter 14 - Ritual for Results .......................................................................................67
Chapter 15 - Acts of Focus..............................................................................................69
Chapter 16 - Using Your Body Centers...........................................................................76
Chapter 17 - Call a Goddess/Saint! ................................................................................78
Chapter 18 - Connect to God Through the Elements ....................................................79
Chapter 19 - Protection ...................................................................................................85
Chapter 20 - In Conclusion .............................................................................................87
APPENDIX 1 – Magical Color Correspondences...........................................................90
APPENDIX 2 – Magical Scent Correspondences ..........................................................92
APPENDIX 3 – Magical Herb Properties ........................................................................95
APPENDIX 4 – Poppet Pattern .....................................................................................105
APPENDIX 5 – Magical Properties of Stones...............................................................106
About the Authors .........................................................................................................109
More Books by the Authors...........................................................................................110

"As above, so below, as the body, so the soul, as the Goddess, so the God, as the Heavens, so the sod."

~~Katrina Rasbold

# Chapter 1 - What is Energy Magic?

Take a moment to sit with each of these particular expressions and see what comes up for you:

*- Freshly mown grass*

*- Newly dug earth*

*- A cool breeze on a hot day*

*- A river or the ocean rushing around your ankles*

*- The majesty of a thunderstorm*

*- The smell of the first few minutes of rain on parched land*

*- A baby's tiny fingers wrapping around your own larger one*

*- The wind in your hair as you ride a magnificent horse*

*- The moment in prayer when you suddenly realize everything will be all right.*

*- The wave of relief that comes when a true miracle, big or small, occurs and you feel that rush of awareness that you are experiencing a blessed moment.*

*- The special feeling that accompanies that miracle where you know that despite all odds, you avoided a tragedy.*

How often do we stand firmly rooted in what we know to be a truly sacred moment, feeling the shivers run over us, and think, "If I could only bottle this energy and save it forever…"? When we are fortunate enough to feel the tingle of those precious moments in life that we want to savor, those that we never want to end, the hair stands up on our necks and on our arms. Our breath catches in our throats and we are momentarily humbled by the power and the pulse of what is happening to us and around us.

What if you really could capture that sacred moment? Would it be any less special? What if you could have more of those moments, even to the point of *that* becoming your norm rather than the ordinary being your standard of living? For that matter, how often is our standard of living simply a feeling of relief that nothing horrible is happening in that moment?

Does that thought cause you to feel as though you would be running between the raindrops? Stealing something you should not be allowed to have? What if you could not only run through the raindrops, but dance through them? What if your mind worked in such a way that even the challenging things that happen in your life felt like blessings that rain down upon you? What if you could feel the power of God or The Goddess or The Universe *right there*, working in every moment of your life? Would *that* not be "true magic?"

Each of the experiences we listed in the first words of this text we were able to rattle off without giving much thought to the process. If we put our minds to it, we could likely come up with twenty, or fifty, or a hundred without a whole lot of effort. We bet you could as well. Pleasure exists all around us, every day, and each is a sacred and holy moment in and of itself.

In fact, in her beautiful poem, *The Charge of the Goddess,* Doreen Valiente writes, "*Let My worship be in the heart that rejoices, for behold, all acts of love and pleasure are My rituals.*" The 100th psalm of the Holy Bible says, "*Make a joyful noise unto the LORD, all ye lands. Serve the LORD with gladness: come before his presence with singing.*" Holy writ after holy writ lets us know, even if through the cracks, that God wants us to be happy and has given us the capacity for tremendous pleasure for a reason.

What we are talking about, however, is something deeper than pleasure. To call these experiences "pleasure" is to minimize their true significance. These are moments when you feel so connected to God and Goddess, to "the Process" that runs through all things, and to our most divine spiritual ecstasy, that it takes your breath right away.

Often, when these flashes of joy come upon us, we enjoy them for a moment, then hurry them away as "reality" once again encroaches. We see them as isolated escapes from the drudgery, fear, and demands that create what we refer to as our lives. Would it not be amazing if it could work the other way around? What would it be like if our divine and holy moments constituted the bulk of our living experience with the occasional dip into mundane life? Would the serenity and pleasure be too much for us to bear or would it be a truly holy and spiritual existence that happens in a world we previously viewed as mundane and ordinary*?*

Would you love to find out for yourself? We did and we can tell you from experience, it is amazing and no, it never gets old and no, we never take it for granted and no, it never, ever lessens in intensity. The wonder never ceases and *it is glorious.*

Those ten moments we described above are not particularly unique or unusual. Most people experience them at some time or another; often many times in their lives or even many times in a year. The internet is filled with common experiences and this is part of what draws us together as a human species. We are nostalgic together when we post in our online social networks about items from our collective pasts that elicit a poignant memory. We bond within our families and circles of friends over shared special memories and what is significant is that *even the very sharing of the memory of those moments* becomes a sacred experience on its own. This demonstrates the power inherent to these experiences: they can procreate into other divine states just by recalling them together. Sharing those memories makes them somehow more corporal and substantial. They then propagate into even more precious moments, born of the original precious moments.

This is the essence of Bio-Universal energy.

Bio-Universal energy is the power behind Energy Magic. Energy Magic is a flow of sacred motion through our lives and even more so, our conscious recognition of its effect, day-by-day and minute-by-minute. It is about creating a purely blessed life by increasing our own awareness of those moments and taking an active role in their development. Energy Magic is about honoring our connection to God and all that is Divine on an ongoing basis. In this process, we step into the holy symphony that goes on around us every day and claim our role in the beautiful music it produces.

Bio-Universal energy is the synergistic blending of our own personal energy. "Bio," refers to "life" or the spirit that exists within us; that indefinable consciousness that makes us inherently who we are. "Universal," in this context, means that with extends beyond our human understanding and dwells in the territory of "God" or "The Universe" or "The Goddess" or "Creator" or whatever it is that a person considers to be divine and holy. *Bio-Universal energy* is the force and *Energy Magic* is the practice we use to channel that force, creating a truly magical experience for those who study and master the art.

When you use Energy Magic to engage Bio-Universal energy, you will begin to notice little improvements every day, right from the beginning. Think about the process of weight loss, for instance. You make conscious changes in your life to live in a more healthful way. Sure, you may not hit your goal in the first month, depending on how far you have to go. Sure, your process will not always be perfect and there will be good days and bad days. If, however, your overall focus and dedication remains strong and you make a determined effort to succeed, your life begins to change on an ongoing basis until eventually, you reach your goal. Even though you did not get there immediately, you quickly began to see changes in how your body looks, feels, and responds. You become stronger. You become progressively lighter. Your internal processes perform more effectively. You begin to receive compliments about your success, even if you are not even close to being finished with your accomplishments.

Energy Magic works the same way. You make improvements to your life on a daily basis and incorporate the practices into your routine. Changes begin to take place right away. You feel different. People begin to notice. Well before you master the techniques and become proficient with Energy Magic, you will experience positive results that change your life in a wonderful way.

God/Goddess/The Universe/The Creator invests in our life experience. More importantly, that force that humans consider holy and sacred waits patiently for us to reach out. When we do, we are greatly rewarded for "coming home." An old Christian song says, *"I've found out if you'll take one step, He'll take two.*" This is how it seems to work. When we reach out to The Universe and call upon God, then God hurries to us and gets busy in our lives. We begin to feel those special, spiritual moments more often. A friend of ours calls it "*being in the zone.*" It is a place where incredible things seem to happen all around you as if *by magic*. It involves a special awareness of how experiences in your life, even those that are challenging or painful, actually happen *for us* rather than *to us*. We are able to objectify our experiences and not collapse into the drama and fear of the moment. When we call to the Goddess, the Goddess comes to us and starts to create a life around us that supports our greatest good.

In our modern society, we have allowed ourselves to become so alienated from that sacred source that it often takes us a while to recognize what is happening. It is like smelling a scent that is familiar to us but we just cannot place. When we begin to incorporate Energy Magic into our lives in a proactive way, we have to trust that just as we cannot see the air around us that we breathe, we cannot always see the hand of God at work in our lives. It is there, whether we see it or not.

# Chapter 2 - Tenets and Terminology of Energy Magic

Energy Magic is non-specific to any particular religion or spiritual path. It is an *individual* process set up to allow each person to create inroads to welcome the presence and direct influence of God/Goddess/The Universe into their life. It is between you and God; no one else. It is about retraining the human mind and spirit to do what it used to do automatically: connect with God/Goddess/Universe/Creator in a meaningful and profound way.

Within this text, you will hear us speak from a Christian perspective as easily as from a Pagan perspective. Both are legitimate connections people establish to communicate with The Divine. We will speak of church and we will speak of circle. When we mention "Energy Magic," it is describing the efforts laid out in this book to combine your own magic with that of what you consider God to be. When we talk about "magic" or "working magic," we mean the act of using our energy and the energy of God to create a positive outcome. When we mention "ritual," it is not from a purely Pagan perspective. Christians have rituals as well. A ritual is simply a series of activities set up in a specific way to create a particular effect. Rituals are typically very symbolic in nature and meaningful to those who participate.

People of all faiths have used energy Magic effectively. Christians, Jews, Pagans, Native Americans, and many other spiritual paths, both mainstream and unconventional, work very effectively with the ideas outlined in this book. The premise of Energy Magic is not about religion, but about *spirituality,* which most people will agree are often vehemently divorced from one another.

Some basic tenets of Energy Magic are important to know and understand. Although it is not essential that each person using Energy Magic embrace all of these ideas as their own, it does help you to know that it is from these standards that the practice is born:

*There is a force in our world, our human experience, that is bigger than we are, that is omniscient, that carries us (sometimes kicking and screaming) toward our own greatest good and overall, to the greatest good of humanity. People give this force different names, but it refers to the power that we each consider sacred and holy.*

*As humans, we contain within us a life force that called our soul or our spirit; an energy that possesses the power of both conscious thought and subconscious processes. It is the place in which free will choices are made and where we actively create the life we will lead. Our spirit is what creates who we are.*

*The energy, force, or Holy Spirit that we sometimes call "God" exists in all things and we feel the power of God in experiences and in expressions of nature.*

*People are ultimately responsible for their own choices and their own behavior. We have the free will choice to seek out God or distance ourselves from God.*

*Psychologically speaking, people respond to certain objects, colors, scents and situations in a conditioned way. While this can be – and often is – individual to the person, there are also common reactions to certain influences that tend to draw us together as a human species.*

*The energy that is "God" makes no mistakes and possesses an understanding and vision that goes beyond our human perception and ability to understand. As humans, we seek to unravel holy mysteries, so since the dawn of time, we have attempted to know the mind and will of God. Even our most enlightened, educated teachers have only been able to catch a glimpse and still cannot fully conceive of all that God is and can do.*

*Even though we are not powerful enough to understand all that is God, we can relate to God just by reaching out and opening our lives to that influence.*

The terminology of Energy Magic can be confusing, so we feel it is important to provide some brief clarification.

We, the authors, honor all paths that people choose to reach out to God as holy and sacred. We have our own path to which we are fully dedicated; however, we honor your path, so long as it is one that brings you to your most sacred self without harming or persecuting to others in the process. Just as we speak different languages in the world, we believe that God also speaks to us in different languages, based on how we will best relate to that holy experience. Jesus said, *"In my father's house, there are many mansions."* God makes room for us all and gives us all the opportunity to live in a sacred and holy way.

Energy Magic celebrates the common sacred feelings and moments in our lives, regardless of the path we choose to reach out to God. It does not deal with the diversity in those paths. There is already too much energy and hatred invested into that pursuit. Instead, Energy Magic is about the joining of different paths in the common experience of welcoming the power of God into our lives and using our own inherent energies to create a sacred and blessed life on this earth.

## When We Say "God," This Is Not Intended As A Gender-Specific Word.

It simply means "that which is holy and sacred" or "the force of spiritual divinity at work in our lives." It does not refer to a male or female gender specification, nor does it refer to the proprietary vision of God from any particular religion.

We could just as easily say, "The Universe," "Creator," or "Goddess" and at times, we will. When we said that God is beyond what we can understand, there is more to the idea than that. As humans, we seek to define God. The easiest way to define God and understand God is to make God more like us. We want relatability and in doing so, we imbue God with human characteristics. For most people, the first impression we had of God was of an old man with a long beard, dressed in white with a hand cupped to his hear, intently making notes about our every prayer.

When we ascribe a human gender onto God of male or female, we are attempting to ascribe relatabilty onto a force that is so far beyond our human understanding that gender does not even exist. Because God is referred to throughout history as male, we often just presume maleness. If, however, God is all powerful, then God can be either male or female or both or neither. If God can talk to people through a burning bush, a cloud, or a donkey, then God can talk to people as a woman. God is formless; therefore, God is anything and everything at one time.

In the past, societies have attempted to relate more strongly to God by creating different faces of God in the form of various Gods and Goddesses. Each God or Goddess had a particular attribute or focus. This distilled the power of God into different arenas. If a woman wanted to pray about her impending childbirth, she would likely feel more comfortable interacting with a female form of God specific to childbirth (such as Brigid) than to a male God. If a man wanted blessings upon the hunt upon which he was about to embark, he would likely feel more comfortable approaching a male God whose focus was on the wooded areas (such as Herne). By creating different faces of God, these people were able to specify their interactions with various aspects of God for their own comfort, especially in a society that was more gender-rigid than our own. It was not God, but humankind, who hated this practice of worshipping God in a different way. God loves us for any attempt we make to get closer.

Where these societies failed is that they went so far in their attempt to humanize God for greater understanding that they assigned to God all sorts of human attributes that are actually weaknesses and frailties in the human process. The mythology of many spiritual paths saddles God with the human frailties of jealousy, pettiness, vengefulness, and, in the polytheistic societies, infidelity, maliciousness, and sloth, among other things. If we accept that God is perfect, then we also must believe that God is above human weaknesses such as these.

We have connected with God through many different spiritual paths and in each instance, we have felt that God is the most divine and pure love a person can ever experience. The only agenda God has to promote is that we live the most blessed and sacred life possible. God seems to expect that during our experience on this earth, that we love one another and honor our connection to the Divine. Even Jesus Christ spoke of two great commandments: *"Thou shalt love the Lord thy God with all thy heart, and with all thy soul, and with all thy strength, and with all thy mind; and thy neighbor as thyself." Luke 10:27*

## Are You Sure?

We have had many people ask us how we can know that the energy we feel and the "God" we experience through multiple spiritual paths is the "real God." In response, we can only say that if a person has to ask, then they have never truly been in and recognized the presence of God. Trust us. There is no mistake. Once you have felt true spiritual ecstasy through the presence of God, you will never mistake anything else for it. We have encountered God full force in Christian churches, in Pagan rituals, in a Native American sweat lodge, in an ashram, and just walking in our own woods. We have heard the voice of God on the radio through a song, on a billboard, and in an off-handed remark made by a child. God is everywhere and *God does not discriminate against those who actively seek out the Divine.*

To that end, you will hear us mention many different venues for connecting with God and will hear us refer to God in many different ways. It is our experience that God follows the old Southern adage of, *"Call me anything but late to supper."* God just wants us there. God does not care what path we take to get there or the name we call out once we are there. Just that we come.

# Chapter 3 - The "Universal" of Bio-Universal

Now that we have established the idea of what God is and what we are, how does Bio-Universal energy tie in at all with baby fingers and rain? The sacred moments in our lives have a specific energy. The goal of Energy Magic is not to reduce those holy experiences down to a mundane level so that they are no longer special. It is instead to elevate the baseline of our day-to-day life to such a point that we live in the sacred and blessed moments on an ongoing basis, regularly connecting with the Divine in an intimate and co-operative fashion.

When we live in a society that requires most of us, on the surface at least, to live a very seemingly ordinary life of work, home, social obligations, how do we bring out the sacred qualities of life? Most of us do not have a life privileged to the point that we can sit serenely in an ashram all day and peacefully contemplate our relationship with the Almighty. Fortunately, there are techniques and props that help us to create a life that is "in the zone" and sacred even while we perform mundane tasks, deal with frustrating people, and go through our daily tasks of life.

There is a saying in the Pagan community that is particularly poignant: *"Live the ordinary life in an extraordinary way."*

That is exactly what we do with Energy Magic. We learn to process events that happen in day-to-day life not as attacks upon us or battles we must fight, but as points of guidance and learning potential. We see experiences not as something that happens *to* us, but as something that happens *for* us.

We have established that God wants us to have a blessed, sacred life and to communicate with the Divine Spirit on a regular basis.

## But Why?

Why would God care whether we are happy? To consider this question and all it entails, we have to actively define God and determine the origin of God. That will establish the motives of God and at that point, we have already gotten into an area that is far beyond the provable and outside of the skill set of humans. In absence of that information, any answer we establish is little more than speculation. We can, however, talk about what *seems* to be so based on our own experiences.

To all appearances, God seems to have an interest in the furthering of the human species. We can extend that thought to say that God has an interest in the furthering of most species because nearly all living creatures possess a will to live and the means to do so barring catastrophe. Our DNA is encoded with the survival of our species and of ourselves by whatever means.

We recently saw a cartoon that had dual frames. In the first frame, an ancient haggard, emaciated man bowed to a Goddess image that was plump and round. In the second frame, a modern plump and round man bowed to the image of a supermodel that was skinny and emaciated. The juxtaposition of those images was the joke, but within it is evidence of how clever our species actually is.

In ancient times when food was scarce, it was important that families have many, many children not only to tend the fields, but also because the threat of premature death was prominent. It was rare for a family to have most of their children survive to adulthood. In those times, the image of beauty was reflected in the fertility goddesses, who were usually plump and healthy to ensure a healthy procreative experience (lots of healthy babies).

Now, we have a population explosion on earth and our image of beauty is an unattainable standard of extremely low body fat. It is a scientific fact that when most women reach a certain level of body fat loss, they will stop ovulating. The idea is that they do not have enough body fat to create reserves to sustain a pregnancy. This is why female athletes will often stop menstruating. At a time when the last thing our planet needs is rampant procreation, our attraction as a species has shifted to a beauty standard of women who cannot reproduce.

Obviously, this is not a conscious shift that human kind elected to take. Much of what we experience and what drives us happens on the inside, far below what our conscious mind can perceive.

Within our human brain there lies an intricate network of receptors called the Pleasure Centers. It was once believed that these were the opioid receptors alone; however, recent studies indicate that this system is far more complex. We are programmed genetically to receive a quota of positive stimulation on a regular basis. When we are in deficit of that quota, we begin to suffer breakdowns in our various systems. This phenomenon is believed to be involved with the process of addiction. Drugs, alcohol, sex, shopping, video games, compulsive overeating, and other addictive behaviors stimulate our pleasure centers. If we are lacking in pleasurable stimulation, our neurological impulses drive us to correct this imbalance, so we go for the quick fixes.

This tells us that we are genetically engineered for the pursuit of joy and pleasure. Since the Creator made us, that means that our Creator wants us to be happy. It is the failing of humankind that we separated ourselves out from our connection to God to the point that it is almost impossible for a lot of us to ever BE truly happy other than in fleeting moments. We live our lives so disconnected from God and Nature that we hardly feel anything anymore except fear and frustration. Remember those ten experiences listed at the beginning of this book?

- *Freshly mown grass*

*- Newly dug earth*

*- A cool breeze on a hot day*

*- A river or the ocean rushing around your ankles*

*- The majesty of a thunderstorm*

*- The smell of the first few minutes of rain on parched land*

*- A baby's tiny fingers wrapping around your own larger one*

*- The wind in your hair as you ride a magnificent horse*

*- The moment in prayer when you suddenly realize everything will be all right.*

*- The wave of relief that comes when a true miracle, big or small, occurs and you feel that rush of awareness that you are experiencing a blessed moment.*

*- The special feeling that accompanies that miracle where you know that despite all odds, you avoided a tragedy.*

Each one is based in a direct interaction with Nature, with God, or both.

When we connect with God/Goddess and the natural flow of life that permeates all things, then a joyful existence is easier to create and maintain. As the old adage goes, *"What you want, wants you."* You want to be happy and happy wants you to have it. When you begin to take steps to make yourself truly happy, even if those are painful and difficult steps, you will be surprised at how the Universe wraps around you and avenues to your success open up.

Having established that God wants us to be happy, the question posed at the beginning of this section remains. *Why?*

The best answer we have is based on the microcosm, the macrocosm, and the Hundred Monkey Theory. The Hundred Monkey Theory is a fascinating premise that originated on the Japanese island of Koshima in 1952. In a study performed on macaque monkeys, scientists worked with two sets of monkeys on separate islands. The monkeys were fond of sweet potatoes and ate them like mad. The scientists introduced bowls of salt water into their environment. At first, the monkeys ignored the salt water because it was not pleasant to drink.

In one of the environments, the scientists showed a couple of the monkeys how to wash their sweet potatoes in the salt water for a different flavor. The monkeys repeated the behavior and other monkeys caught on. The behavior spread. In the other environment where the monkeys were not shown how to wash their sweet potatoes, they continued to ignore the water.

According to the scientists, the "hundredth monkey" to wash his sweet potato in salt water represented a "critical mass consciousness" and the monkeys in the second environment (an island away, in fact) who previously ignored the salt water spontaneously began washing their sweet potatoes in salt water.

The scientists speculated that the collective animal consciousness of the hundred monkeys caused the remote monkeys to connect with the brain waves of the hive mind and act accordingly.

Like all good psychological theories, there were eventually those who denounced the findings and poked holes in the theories. We have studied psychology long enough to know that *any* theory can be discredited given the appropriate motivation and pre-existing bias. Much like religion and politics, the factions in psychology are hotly polarized to the point that immediate lack of credibility is presumed if a study comes from an opposing faction. There are many examples in the animal kingdom of animals seeming to read one another's minds from a distance and respond in tandem. There is also the very apt musing of the Old Bard himself who said, *"There are more things in heaven and earth, Horatio, than are dreamt of in your philosophy."*

If we, as the individual microcosms of the human race, make a concerted effort to become more enlightened, sacred people (note we did not say "religious" people) and as a result, become happier, kinder people, does that not then further the entirety of the human race toward that critical mass consciousness? If it does not and the whole thing is a myth, what have we lost if we, in fact, made ourselves enormously happy?

Why does God want us to be happy? If we are happy, we are part of the tilting balance that takes the whole human race *toward* a more spiritual, loving, and sacred existence and *away from* a critical mass that is mired in fear and frustration. *What we want, wants us.* We just have to make the inroads to receive.

Many religions formed around the idea of exclusively receiving and the relationship between God/The Universe and humans as a one-way street. Many sacred texts tell us that we must act in accord and *"The Lord helps those who help themselves."* In Energy Magic, we contribute our own energy to the process of manifestation by harnessing the energy of our own free will and directing it toward our goal in tandem with the blessings from the Universe.

# Chapter 4 - The "Bio" of Bio-Universal

Each of us has two selves that govern our day-to-day lives. Between the two of them, they create our personality. They house our fears, our wisdom, our truths, our motivations, and our potentials for success and failure. One is the Conscious Self, which is our perceived thought process, emotions, and awareness. The other is our Higher Self, which is our subconscious mind and innermost functions. Higher Self is able to tap into knowledge and insight that is not normally available to Conscious Self. Higher Self is a calm, relaxed part of your being that is able to research, learn, and absorb information that Conscious Self is too busy and distracted to handle.

Conscious Self is more involved with "doing" and "reacting" while Higher Self is more involved with "knowing" and "assimilating." Conscious Self reacts to situations. Higher Self integrates them, accepts them as a part of the intricate weave of your life path and isolates specific learning opportunities for the Conscious Self to acknowledge and absorb. Imagine that Higher Self processes an experience, then writes up a summary report with certain sections highlighted for emphasis, and puts it in the inbox of Conscious Self.

For most people, the inbox gets pretty full because Conscious Self is so busy "putting out fires" and problem solving during our hectic, mundane life that it doesn't even go into the office, much less look at the inbox.

Higher Self is able to process information on a more esoteric, "bigger picture" level than Conscious Self. Conscious Self often becomes confused by the weather of emotions and by external stimulation that accompanies our day to day life. Conscious Self has trouble figuring out what is important and what is incidental and irrelevant.

Higher Self is not influence or intimidated by concepts such as "I can't…," "But what if…," and "I want…" With the external and internal flotsam and jetsam cleared away, Higher Self is able to view a situation from a very simple and realistic manner. It assimilates the experience through the panoramic process of understanding our past and predicting our future, based on an intricate dance of intuition and predictive summations from past behaviors. Higher Self can analyze the experience and reasonably predict the impact it will have on you and others and formulate a greatest and best outcome.

Higher Self is sort of like a Global Positioning System that talks to you: "Turn right at your next stop to reach your destination." If we fail to pay attention and do not turn right, it says, "Enter the left lane and make a U turn at the next light, then turn left at light after that" or "Turn right at your light, then right at the first turn after that." Our Higher Self constantly adjusts its wisdom and guidance based on experiences we have and choices we make.

Higher Self is able to see through to the true nature of an event or set of circumstances and dispassionately evaluate the event's place and purpose on your life path.

Although it was likely once different for humankind, for the average person, the Conscious Self is only aware of information provided by Higher Self on an occasional basis, such as when we are stunned by flashes of insight or "hunches." Our goal with Energy Magic is to reacquaint our estranged selves with one another to work cooperatively to create a balanced and insightful life.

## Where Is The Higher Self?

Our brain is measurable both in mass and in the electrical impulses that it generates to keep us alive and cognitive. Because it can be located and measured, it is easier to study. Our Conscious Self consists of a vast network of sensory, emotional, and neural impulses. Although we have made great strides in our understanding of how the brain functions, what we actually know is little more than the tip of the iceberg. It is leagues beyond what we knew a hundred years ago and yet very basic concepts like "Why do we dream?" elude us. There is still so much to learn about the processes that combine to create our behaviors our conscious thoughts. In a world filled with technology and knowledge that far surpasses what anyone could have imagined even ten years ago, there are still more questions than answers in the neurology field.

As sparse as our education is about Conscious Self, it vastly overshadows the tiny modicum of information we have about Higher Self, which is still mostly speculation based on personal experience. In either instance, we are still routinely shocked at the vehement denial "professionals" express when they encounter a theory that supports any sort of esoteric or spiritual premise. The attitude is typically, "No, it can't be that. I don't know what it is, but it's not *that*."

For thousands of years, humankind has attempted to prove the existence of a soul or spirit inside the body and to find where it resides within us. The medical profession has sought to explain the fact that a person's physical weight is less immediately following death than it was minutes before death. Dr. Duncan McDougall of Haverill, Massachusetts conducted extensive experiments weighing bodies before, during and immediately after death. His body of evidence convinced him that a soul weighs approximately 21 grams. *The New York Times* and *American Medicine* (a medical journal) published his work and other medical professionals immediately went on the attack. Just like with those monkeys, the opposing factors descended. The debate focused on details of his methodology for collecting information rather than on the validity of his conclusions and as such, the loss of weight, now an accepted fact, was never explained. Again, it fell to "I don't know what it is, but it isn't *that.*"

## The Chakras, The Meridians, and The Lymphatic System

Energy workers accept that we have seven power points lined up in our bodies: the chakra points. These energy centers regulate the flow of energy into and through the body. Energy meridians connect the chakra points and act as the vessels that circulate the energy throughout our bodies. The lymphatic system is essential to the release of excessive or unhealthy energy that builds up in this intricate network and acts as a series of "exit points" for the discharge of this energy. You can see how closely our energy processing system mirrors our nutrient processing system. The chakra points are like tiny hearts for different kinds of energy. The meridians are like our blood vessels and arteries. The lymphatic system is like our bladder and kidneys. The difference is that we are processing energy instead of oxygen and food nutrients.

These chakra points, energy meridians, and the flow of Bio-Universal energies into, through, and out of our bodies are vital to our health on all three levels: spirit, mind, and body. This triad must be in balance to reach our maximum health potential. When any one of these three is compromised, the other two suffer as well. Just as we have to care for our bodies to achieve maximum health, we also have to care for our minds and our spirits. Balance is essential; otherwise, all the hard work we do to benefit the body will only result in partial success.

## The Aura

We also have an "aura" that emanates from our bodies, normally unseen by the naked eye. This is our own electromagnetic field that radiates our personal energy into the world. It creates our "bubble" of personal space around us. Many people are able to train themselves to see the auras of the people around them. It is a similar process as training oneself to see the 3-D pictures in Magic Eye artwork. As with Magic Eye pictures, once you see the aura, it becomes difficult to not see it. It is simply a way of adjusting the vision and training yourself to see in a different way. Our auras change according to our mood and our health on all levels. Auras are thought to be another place where the soul or Higher Self lives.

## The Third Eye

'The "third eye" is a concept embraced by many cultures. It is associated with the brow chakra, which you see in purple in the diagram above. Friar Richard Rohr speculates that "first eye" is what we perceive with the five physical senses. "Second eye" is our reasoning and reflection. "Third eye" goes further and is, as Rohr puts it, "Having the mind of Christ." It is a coming together of sacredness that puts one in a very holy and receptive state of mind. Many yoga paths use the third eye for inner focus. The Hindu people honor the inner guru by placing a dot of red sandalwood on the brow or Ajna (Aadnyaa) chakra. Their interpretation of this chakra means "command center." When a person closes their eyes and the distraction of visual stimulation is removed, often their eyes automatically shift upward with their "vision" directed toward the area of the third eye. (Go on, try it. Relax, close your eyes and see what they do.)

The third eye is thought to refer to the pineal gland, a tiny part of our endocrine system embedded deeply between the two hemispheres of the brain, surrounded by a web of carotid arteries. Its location tracks directly back into the brain from the center of the forehead, generally considered to be the "third eye" point. Philosopher René Descartes studied the pineal gland with great interest and referred to it as "the principal seat of the soul." The 19th century Christian mystic, Max Heindel theorized that the human pituitary and pineal gland were much more active in the past and "when man was in touch with the inner worlds, these organs were his means of ingress thereto." Other theorists have joined with his notions that these essential glands are very dormant versions of the ones that operated in our ancestors.

The pineal gland now controls some of our most important functions. It is responsible for releasing melatonin and therefore, governing our circadian rhythms. This is accomplished through the pineal gland's interpretation of light and darkness, which in and of itself is a concept with mystical overtones. A disruption in the health of the pineal gland can result in sleep disorders and bipolar disorder. A minor example of disrupted circadian rhythms is the effect of jet lag.

Where does Higher Self live? To answer that question, we consider the limited results that literally thousands of years of study and speculation have produced about the soul from some of our most enlightened masters. We must then conclude that this intricate circuitry of the energy system described above comes together to constitute a secondary body energy system within our physical bodies wherein lies our Higher Self, pulsing and working every bit as hard as our more tangible, observable and therefore, measurable body organs and systems.

## Marrying Up the Selves Again

The goal of Energy Magic is bridge the gap between the Conscious Self and the Higher Self. We do believe that full integration is likely possible with tremendous dedication over a long period; however, even a partial reconnect provides tremendous benefits to those who make the effort. This separation of the two selves is an evolutionary development and as Max Heindel proposed, it is likely that the dormant pineal gland and the pituitary gland likely played a more significant role in joining those two awarenesses in prior human culture.

Human life as a macrocosm moves through various cycles of development, just as the microcosms (each human life) cycle through different phases. We can track through history the progression of human interest and involvement away from a purely spiritual focus toward a purely scientific focus. This shift from faith and spirit to science and intellect is often maligned by the religious sector but is actually a progressive evolution. Humans, both individually and collectively, work in cycles and in the case of humankind, those cycles tend to cover many years, even centuries. Our current focus on science has provided us with many opportunities and benefits that have furthered our progress. This time we have spent prioritizing the measurable, scientific aspect of life is not necessarily the evil it has been made out to be, nor is it absolute salvation.

Imagine that rather than just a linear progression, our time between these two extremes is a pendulum:

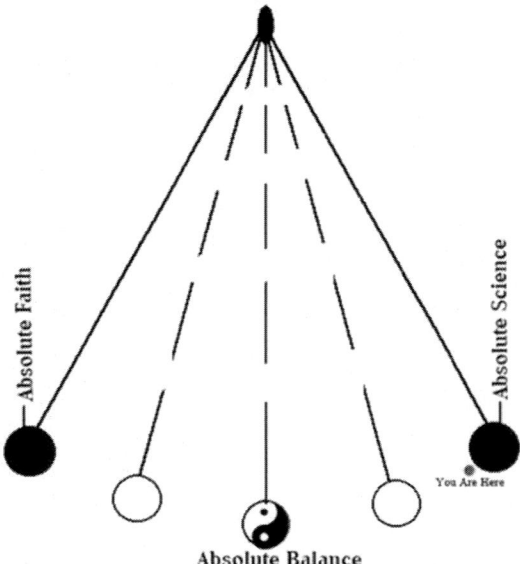

We swing into the immersion of absolute faith, spirituality, and religion and then we swing into the immersion of absolute science, academia, and logic. Each of these has its profound contribution and each has its tremendous detriment, namely, a society nearly devoid of progress in the opposite field.

It is important to note that we said *progress* in the opposite field rather than a life devoid of the *influence* of that opposite field. We do not lose what we gained during that previous cycle. We simply do not have an emphasis on further progression. Ideally, we would live in a time that is a perfect balance between the two and in human existence, we have enjoyed several of those balance periods. We can bemoan the loss of emphasis on our preferred side; however, it is important to note that the fluctuations are inevitable. Humans cycle. That is the reality of it. The trick is to maximize the benefits from each extreme.

At this point, our impression is that we are moving away from a time of the purely scientific approach and are moving to a more faith-based platform. Many intelligent, stable people are looking for a new way to connect to God, feeling that the established paths have failed them. Some are clinging to paths that do not work for them simply to have some sort of connection to the holy and sacred. At a time when life is difficult on many levels and there appears to be a great deal of unfairness and imbalance in the world, it is natural to look to a higher power for answers. Anytime we are in the full power of one side, we will inevitably crave the opposite side. We have to wonder if the craving humans now feel for a quality connection to their Higher Power will cause our pineal and pituitary glands to blink back into action and return to greater activity as this transition occurs.

Although the Conscious Self and Higher Self do have difficulty communicating, there are certain activities that allow them to bridge that gap, if only for short periods. When we are dreaming, for instance, Higher Self uses talking points from the experiences of Conscious Self to work through inner conflict. In dreams, we usually process information in symbolic form rather than literal translation. Symbols and images are a common language between the Conscious and Higher Selves. Whereas there was likely a time in history when we could access Higher Self just as easily as we reach Conscious Self, we now have to create specific circumstances to allow them to communicate. This is how divorced these two sacred and vital selves are from one another at this point in human development. Because of the similarities in the brainwaves to dreaming, meditation is another of those self-created moments that bridges the chasm between Conscious Self and Higher Self.

Energy Magic is about re-introducing those sacred selves to one another and teaching them to communicate on a regular basis. This creates that "in the zone" feeling and puts you in that perfect balance between the two selves. It is essential to realize that Higher Self and Conscious Selves are equally essential. One is no more important or desirable than the other and each needs the other to function appropriately. Just like with the cycles of human focus, the ideal situation is a perfect balance between the Conscious and Higher Selves.

In addition to symbols, another common language between the two selves is color. People have psychological reactions to different colors, both individually and as a species. For individuals, the reaction is more of a conditioned response. For the species, this collective response is typical to most humans. Prisons and hospitals, for instance, are rarely painted red or bright yellow. Those are colors that excite and sometimes agitate people. Most commonly, mint greens, pastel blues and soft earth tones are used because they are calming. The colors become symbols that cause both the Conscious Self and the Higher Self to react in a certain way without Conscious Self needing to translate out the message from Higher Self. It is as though the program is circumnavigated and you went straight in for the hard-wiring.

God/The Goddess/The Universe/Creator speaks to us through our Higher Selves. Sometimes, we will see something through our Conscious Selves that causes an immediate reaction in our Higher Selves.

Once, Katrina was driving while worrying on an issue that had plagued her for a few weeks. She had prayed about it and sent energy toward the resolution, but kept coming back to the idea that she could do more; that she should have seen results by that time. At that moment, she drove past a church and the sign out front said, "Do not dig up in doubt what you planted in faith." The hairs went up on the back of her neck. It was as though God spoke to her directly through Conscious Self and gave her the answer she needed. As advised by the sign, she let go of her control of the situation she had been concerned about and it quickly righted itself. There are times when the message is so loud and clear that it cannot be missed.

We all have stories like those. A song on the radio, a billboard, a chance comment even by a stranger can sound like the word of God in our ears and guess what? It is. When we accept this process as an ongoing reality rather than an isolated coincidence, we begin to tune in deeper and receive guidance from God that we would otherwise overlook. That is another effect of Energy Magic. If we disconnect from Higher Self, we disconnect from the part of ourselves that is most responsive to the God's influence. This, in turn, causes us to disconnect from God.

As you further your practice of Energy Magic and activate that Bio-Universal energy in your daily life, you will begin to find that insights come more easily. Ideas that feel more like "original thought" occur spontaneously rather than all thoughts manifesting as just another link in the ongoing thought chain of the day. These are your guidance from God and your blessings.

Just like any other kind of exercise, you will begin to flex the "muscles" that tune into Bio-Universal energy and use it on an ongoing basis for your greatest good. You will forge better and stronger communication between your Higher Self and your Conscious Self and this will bring you closer to God. You will feel the influence of God more easily in your life and will begin to feel at one with the concert of natural energy in life. Miracles will begin to show up out of nowhere to the point that you will forget what it is like to *not* live a miraculous life. Opportunities for success will manifest seemingly from nowhere. When you need to make a choice, it will be easier for you to see which path is ultimately the most advantageous. It is like tuning directly into a frequency that previously had only fuzzy reception.

# Chapter 5 - About Energy

We have discussed the "Universal" energy of God a good bit and have talked about how energy moves through your body in a system similar to our own circulatory and excretory systems. Now, we will look at some of the specific properties of energy and its movement potentials.

We have determined that the overall slant of Universal energy is toward our own greatest good. God wants us to be happy and successful. God also wants us to learn particular lessons that will take us to a happier and more successful life. Sometimes, we ignore the gentle nudges of those lessons and God has to take a stronger approach. The guidance of God is not always what we want to hear or experience, but it is always in our best interest. The beauty of Energy Magic is that it puts us in closer touch with what God is telling us so we can make changes before those gentle nudges become full-scale beatings.

The energy that is inside all of us, the personal energy that joins with the energy of God when we do specific work toward bettering our lives, starts out as neutral. All of us want to better our lives, at least presumably. Part of the free will that God grants us, however, renders our energy neutral – neither good nor bad – until we color it with our own intention. It is our own motivation and intent, nothing more, that determines whether the energy we set into motion with our own will is positive or negative.

The energy that we use to change our lives is similar to the energy we use in our day-to-day life and call electricity. As with electricity, there are ways to speed it up or amplify it and ways to slow it down or ground it. The energy that flows through the wiring of your house has no intention or will. It is simply energy. It can cook our food or it can kill a person in an electric chair. A person directs that energy when they throw the switch and completes the circuit. Similarly, with Bio-Universal energy, it is the will of the person, the practitioner, which determines whether the work you do with the energy is dark or light, good or bad.

When our electricity stops, what do we normally say? "The power is out." Electricity is energy and that is power. It is the power to create the outcomes we wish to see, such as a light coming on or our TV bringing us entertainment. Bio-Universal energy is also power. We can throw the switch and open up to it on an ongoing basis, but also channel it into specific goals when we have a need to do so.

# Chapter 6 - The Power of Intention

A specific energy comes over us when we earnestly pray. We cannot duplicate the feeling involved in that connection with God/Goddess in any other experience *except in those experiences where we appeal to God in other forms*. It is the connection with God and the *congress* with God that creates that specific type of interactive energy. Anyone who has ever truly been in the presence of God can tell you that there is nothing like it.

Prayer is one of the means of connecting with God and is certainly the most socially acceptable means. A Shaman who is meditating connects to God. A Wiccan who is creating and enacting a protection spell connects to God/Goddess. A Catholic who recites the liturgy connects to God. A Muslim who bows in the direction of Mecca and prays connects to God. A Buddhist monk connects to God. All experience similar sensations and typically, similar results. The key that opens the door to this connection is *what awakes the spiritual connect to God for this one person.*

For any of these people, *the integrity of their intent* is what is vital to the outcome. In our efforts to qualify and judge a person's interaction with God as worthy or acceptable, there is a huge push to be "right." As you have likely gathered from the wording of this book, Energy Magic does not accept the implication that one person's interaction with God is "right" while another's is "wrong." To us, right and wrong are extensions of the intent of the person who is praying or connecting to God. Consider the circumstances below. Who is ethical and who is not?

> *A Pagan ("person of the earth," meaning someone of a nature based religion who is not a Christian) who connects to God by way of spell work to help a neighborhood family find a safe and affordable home?*
>
> *A Christian minister who prays for the homosexuals and Pagans in his community to be eliminated?*
>
> *A Witch who mixes herbs together and prays over them to heal a friend who has a fever?*
>
> *A Christian who goes to church every Sunday, does fund-raising for the schools, but is unfaithful to her husband and is a closet kleptomaniac?*
>
> *A Pagan who casts a spell to get her boss to fall in love with her against his will?*
>
> *A Christian who prays that God will help him become the person he wants to be and attract a lifetime marriage partner?*
>
> *A Druid who honors the astrological passages, honors the earth through tremendous efforts toward ecology, and uses personal energy to force his father to changes his will so that his inheritance is larger.*

*A Christian who believes that we are put on this earth to emulate Jesus Christ and as a result, cares for the sick and the homeless, teaches English as a second language, and donates to the local battered women's shelter.*

The point of this exercise is to say that no one is "good" or "bad" simply because of the spiritual path they follow to connect to God/The Universe/Goddess. It is *personal intent* and how that intent manifests into action and form in the outside world that colors the integrity of a person, regardless of their faith. We have all known people who considered themselves Godly, but who commit atrocious acts, often in God's name. We have all known people who were maligned by others, but who worked aggressively to make the world a better place.

The energy within us is neutral. The energy that comes from The Divine is, by nature, directed toward our own greatest good. We can use our own bio-energy to accentuate the existing flow of energy that comes from God and take us toward our greatest good at a much faster, cleaner progression. Likewise, we can use our own bio-energy to fight against the flow toward our greatest good, argue with God about how our lives should be, and slow down the process of getting there. It is up to us how we use our own personal energy and that is the very specific and directed power of free will.

Remember the idea that *"Energy is power"* and that electricity, as energy, can be used to harm or to heal? Again, the intent is vital to the outcome.

As you can see and as you likely already surmised, there are good people and misguided people and downright hateful people on every spiritual path. After a lifelong study of various religions, we can say with a certain degree of experienced assurance that no one religious path that attracts a holier or a more wretched type of human than does another. You might as well look at different roads leading to the same destination and imagine that there are roads that only good people travel and road that only bad people travel. What matters is the heart of the person and whether their intent is born from a position of love or a position of hate. Does it come, from a position of openness or a position of greed? What matters is whether a person is praying to make himself or herself a better person or to change someone else to meet their own dictates of how the world should be.

God knows our heart and God knows our intent. As we discussed, God's agenda is toward our own greatest good. The interesting part is that God's view of our life is more panoramic than our own. We can see our position in life and in a set of circumstances from our own limited perspective. God can see how this situation affects us in the end, how it bleeds over into other aspects of our lives and the options that we cannot even foresee. It is not at all unusual for God to have a whole different idea of what is best for us than what *we* think is best for us.

Energy Magic is about connecting with God in a meaningful way and learning more about ourselves so that we can create the most positive outcome to any given situation. Another side of Energy Magic is that once we have taken measures to commune with God effectively over any given situation, we can have absolute faith that however the situation is resolved, it will be for our own greatest good.

Some have called Energy Magic a form of "proactive prayer." Prayer tends to be a passive activity. We connect with God and ask for what we want and then we wait for it to happen. When using Energy Magic, we take an approach that is closer to *"pray for help, but keep rowing for the shore."* We believe that God *"helps those who help themselves."* We embrace a very active engagement with God to create the best possible resolution. We believe *"as above, so below,"* meaning that just as we move energy to create a specific outcome, we also "act in accord" and do the mundane legwork as well, knowing that the outcome is assured and blessed.

## A Brief Recap

The next part of our exploration of Energy Magic will focus on its specific practice. Before we move forward into the "how to" of the process, it is important to internalize some highlights of the first part of this book.

Take a breath. Open your mind, your heart, and your spirit. Take a moment to release, even temporarily, the conditioned about typical communication with God. Read these ideas again:

> *God wants us to be happy and successful.*
>
> *God can see more than we can see about our current circumstances and ourselves*
>
> *God wants us to connect and have a holy, spiritual life.*
>
> *God sees beyond race, creed, religion, sex, and all other earthly manifestations of who we are and into our true spirit.*
>
> *God is everywhere.*
>
> *There is a sacred energy to all things and God exists in all expressions of nature.*
>
> *People connect to God in individual ways.*
>
> *Our own energy is neutral until we color it with our own intent and motivation.*
>
> *Energy is a power that we can use to heal or to decimate, to create or to destroy.*
>
> *God gave us free will to decide how we will use our spiritual energy.*
>
> *Certain environmental experiences can elicit a greater closeness to God.*

*Humans have a Conscious Self that is our awake and aware perception and a Higher Self that is our sacred, spiritual connection.*

*We have the freedom to use our own sacred and self-generated energy in any way we choose.*

*Our own choices for using that energy define whether we become a positive or a negative contributor to the human experience.*

*The degree to which we work with the positive flow from God determines how quickly and cleanly we get to our own greatest good on an ongoing basis.*

Regarding our own intent, we can lie to ourselves, we can lie to others, but we cannot lie to The Universe. Ultimately, our true colors and intentions come through and we are always accountable for how we use our personal energy for manifestation. This is the true nature of karma. The Universe does not negotiate and knows our every intent and action. It is simple cause and effect. We can slow down or speed up our passage toward Greatest Good by our own behavior. We can slow down or speed up the efficiency of Bio-Universal energy by using certain tools and practices as well.

# Chapter 7 - Properties of Energy – What Speeds It Up?

Try to retrain your mind to see the spiritual energy that is processed through your chakra system, transported through your meridian system, then cleansed, and purified by your lymphatic system as **actual energy**. Remember the law of energy conservation: *"Energy cannot be created or destroyed, only converted from one form to another."* When you are born, you have a soul/spirit. That spirit has energy that is your own personal "bio" energy. The energy seeks changed into form.

That being the case, there are conductors to energy and there are resistors to energy. Energy recognizes certain factors that will speed it up and help it move faster and others that slow it down or ground it. We can use these properties to focus and speed up our spiritual connection. If we want to move electricity, we will use a conductor such as metal or water that we know is energy receptive and directive. If we do not want electricity to move, we use a grounding agent such as earth, rubber, or other materials that stop the flow. It is the same with Bio-Universal energy.

We have all used the phone during a "bad" connection. "Can you hear me now?" We repeat ourselves, we move to different areas, or even try phoning back again to get a better connection. The connection exists, but we cannot get our thoughts conveyed because of interference of one kind or another on the line. The goal when using Energy Magic is to create an environment and mindset where our calls go right through every time and are loud, crisp, and clear. We want the energy we direct toward a goal to be as strong as it can be and to move quickly toward its target. When you have become adept at using Bio-Universal energy, God has a bat phone and you are Commissioner Gordon.

Some people call this "magic," because it works like magic. From thought and words, form becomes manifest. Just like a magician on a stage who pulls something from nowhere, so do we manifest positive outcome purely from our connection to God. Something that was not in our lives before is now there or something that was in our lives before is now gone because of our energy investment.

The explanation we like best for the word "magic" in this:

## *Make A Generative and Interesting Change*

The operative words here are, of course, "generative" (having the power or function of generating, originating, producing, or reproducing) and "interesting" (because if it's boring, who cares?").

Every time we pray, we change our lives in some way. If our efforts fail, we learn that what we want was not in the interest of our greatest good. If our efforts are successful, change our lives through the generative nature of our answered prayer. Regardless, change occurs.

Our goal is to make that change something lovely and *interesting*. It is one way of connecting to God and sending energy toward a goal. It is one of the forms of Energy Magic.

There are very specific ways of praying that will convey our intentions clearly. By praying, we mean "engaging God/Goddess in a meaningful way." Of course, God understands our hearts and what we want to do and say. The Lord loves drunks, little children, and people who struggle with words and intent.

It is for our OWN benefit that we must be specific. The "universal" part of "Bio-Universal" is completely literate on what we wish to accomplish. The "bio" part has to engage both the Higher Self and the Conscious Self and get both of those two feisty horses to pull the cart in the right direction.

Our goal in praying is to secure the clearest, most efficient connection we can between our own energy and that of Deity, then amplify the energy as much as possible and direct it toward our goal. To do this, we must fully court the Higher Self and coax it into a handshake with the Conscious Self, then get them to work together. Their job is then to engage Deity fully and completely and move the energy into the direction where you choose to send it.

The following pointers can greatly assist our own Higher Self in relating to our Conscious Self to get them on the same page and working together effectively toward your goal.

## The Art of Ritual

Ritual is a word that many people shy away from thinking it is about congress with the devil. Having a ritual sounds sinister and spooky. A ritual is nothing more than a specific set of actions, performed for their symbolic value. Often, a ritual is nothing more than a behavior repeated throughout life. When a Christian congregation sings the Doxology or passes the offering plate, that is a ritual. When you blow out the candles on your birthday cake or put a star on top of the Christmas tree, that is a ritual. The words "ritual" and "tradition" are tightly related.

The sole purpose of ritual is to focus our intent and our energy, so it is an important part of Energy Magic. In ritual, there is a specific flow and procedure and every act is deliberate and meaningful. As the definition implies, there is a great deal of symbolism to your actions when working in ritual. Remember that the Higher Self responds favorably to symbolism, so ritual is a means to access the place where God speaks. That is why most religious ceremonies are rife with ritual. Done correctly, it takes us into Higher Self.

Very nearly every time we work with Energy Magic, we will perform a ritual of some kind. Ritual is very personal and adaptable. There is no hard and fast set of rules for how you conduct your own ritual. Examples are in this text; however, you are always free to modify according to your own pleasure or interest.

When you conduct a ritual, you should consider where it will happen and properly prepare the area.

**Secure the area.** When you are going to connect with God, interruptions can be distracting. This is a sacred and protected time, so it is up to you to honor it by breaking away from your busy schedule and reducing distractions so that you can focus. If you are not alone in the area you will use, let people who are with you know that you are going to be praying (or insert your favorite appropriate word instead) and you need privacy for X amount of time. Turn off or disconnect phones. Make certain pets are self-sufficient for the time being.

**Prepare the area.** We will talk about how to create your own sacred space and altar area. You can work inside, outside, or where ever you choose. The area should be free of any hazards. If you are barefoot and outside, for instance, check for glass or sticks that could hurt your feet. Decide what materials you will need for your ritual time and get them within easy access. The following topics will teach you about specific props and circumstances to accentuate your ritual and ritual area and heighten your connection to Higher Self. This will give you ideas for how to further prep your ritual area to create a sacred environment that best nourishes your spirit and your connection to God/Goddess.

You will see as we progress through the suggestions that the primary triggers are in sensory perception and common sense. Triggers are specific sensory perception devices that elicit a particular reaction in us and that reaction often amplifies our personal energy.

## Colors

We have discussed the way our brains react automatically to a few specific colors. In the appendices of this book, you will find a list of color affiliations. These account for the typical feelings evoked by certain colors and so we use those colors in our ritual presentation to heighten those feelings. These properties reflect the vibrations created in humans by those colors. You may have your own conditioned responses to certain colors and that may affect your selection. Your color selection affects the altar cloth you use, candle color, any small bags used to contain tokens or charms, your own clothing, and any other tools you might use.

## Herbs and Scents

Spiritual paths have used smoldering herbs, resins, roots, essential oils, and incenses throughout recorded history. There is little doubt that the sense of smell is one of the most powerful mood setters in existence for humans. The smell of bread baking, chocolate, freshly cut grass, and certain colognes or after shave, and other personal triggers will quickly affect your mood and even your thoughts.

We have known for thousands of years that certain smells create specific reactions in humans. Aromatherpy did not exist by that name even a hundred years ago, yet humans knew that they could burn items to create scent and use that power to elicit a physical or emotional response. A French chemist named Rene-Maurice Gattefosse coined the phrase "aromatherapy" in 1937. A French surgeon named Jean Valnet later pioneered the use of essential oils in medicine because of the reactions the scents caused in his patients.

Our response to scent in ritual is both physical and emotional. If, for instance, your mother ever rubbed your chest with Vapo-rub when you were little, the smell of eucalyptus may be especially soothing to you now when you have a cold. There is a physical reaction because eucalyptus has the healing property of opening up the sinuses and promoting drainage. There is also an emotional reaction of nostalgia. In Energy Magic, we work with both reactions as they come, optimizing the choice of herbs based on our own emotional reaction and the properties that are natural to the scent.

There are several ways to create a pleasing scent that promotes your goals when you are planning your ritual:

**Incense** – There are many incenses available on the market and most are relatively inexpensive. Incense are made as sticks, cones, or powders. There books on how to make your own incenses as well.

**Resins** – Copal, amber, frankincense, and myrrh are among the resins that can be burned on small, round, self-igniting charcoal briquettes. **These are a different kind of charcoal briquette from the ones you use in your barbeque**. Barbeque charcoal must never be burned inside. The correct types of charcoals look like these:

These types of briquettes continually spark you light them and constantly reignite themselves. You can burn powdered incenses, herbs, scented oils, or resins on them very effectively. A little goes a long way, so start out with a small amount of scent and add more if needed.

**Scented candles -** Some candles have a strong scent pitch and can provide a pleasing aroma for your ritual area.

**Oils –** There are essential oils, which are pure oils extracted from the source. and there are scented oils, which are essential oils placed in a carrier oil like grape seed oil or sweet almond oil). Essential oils are usually more expensive, but last longer because they are pure and uncut. You may use oils to anoint yourself or your tools. You can place oils in a diffuser or an oil burner to scent your area. You may also place a drop or two on one of the self-igniting charcoals mentioned above.

**Potpourri –** Potpourri is a collection of fragrant herbs, oils, and spices that you place in a container to provide fragrance in an area. You can also cover potpourri with boiling water and heat it on a special potpourri burner. The scent will carry on the steam that releases from the heat.

In the appendices of this book, you will find a very brief reference list of certain scents and their properties. In our previous example, for instance, if you wanted to create a healing ritual for a friend who is ill, you might use a eucalyptus-based scent to increase the healing energy around you and through you. If you are working to bring love in your life, you could use a rose scent. If you wanted to attract money to you, you would use a spice-based scent.

The second use of herbs and flowers in ritual is for a visual effect. A flower bouquet is a lovely addition to the altar area for a spring ritual to welcome the warmer temperatures. Harvest altars often have wheat or corn on them.

Yet another use lies in the medicinal property of the herb or flower itself. There are many wonderful books on the medicinal and magical properties of plants and herbs. In the oft mentioned Appendices at the end of the book, we will include a very brief reference for your benefit. In a later chapter, we will discuss how these herbs and flowers may be used within the ritual itself. My own favorite herb books are *The Master Book of Herbalism* by Paul Beyerl and *Cunningham's Encyclopedia of Magical Herbs* by Scott Cunningham.

## Sound

The use of various sounds and music in ritual is very nearly universal throughout spiritual paths. Most religions have their own preferred music and sounds for different effects. This is also a highly individualized field. You have heard people say, "My feet just won't behave!" when they hear a particular song. We hear a song from our past and we are briefly taken back in time. A particularly poignant song can have us in tears or a happy one can compel us to dance. *"Music soothes the savage beast."* There is little denying that music and sound are factors that affect our mood, or mindset, and our ability to focus.

Some people enjoy chanting, some like heavy percussion, others like techno, and some like New Age music. Some people like to do their spiritual work in complete silence. There is no "wrong" choice of sound. You can play recorded music or create your own. You can softly beat on a drum and meditate to the entrancing sound. The sounds around you during spiritual work create an emotional impact and affect your own energy movement and direction. We would not do our spiritual work while a car alarm is going off a few feet away from us or a dog is barking incessantly. Such sounds would be a tremendous distraction and take away from our energy flow.

Take some time – and perhaps a trip through YouTube – to gauge your reaction to different types of sounds

## Entering a Trance State

Like the word "ritual," "trance" is a word that has gotten a very bad reputation. When you do trance work, you do not lose control of your mind. Tracing is a type of meditation in which you respond to music, activity, or other stimulation in such a way that you enter into an altered state. Your visual stimulation might begin to fade away as you go further inside your own mind during the trance. Far from losing control of your mind, which seems to be the baseless fear, you are actually more in control of your mind and can easily access Higher Self. We achieve a trance state by many methods, but the most common are dancing, fire gazing, drumming, chanting, humming, listening to music, and meditating.

Trancing is not usually something that happens to a person right away or to a novice. "Talking in Tongues," which is a practice common to Pentecostal religions, is a form of trance. Some deep meditations qualify as trances. Some people who pray the rosary, a Catholic practice, will pray themselves in a trance. Trances are common in situations of sensory deprivation. They sometimes take place in sweat lodges of Native American practice. The basic hallmark is that what is around you in your sensory perception fades and you begin to have an altered perception. This is not usually a drug-induced experience. Properly done, this can result in a near perfect communion with your Higher Self.

## The Spoken and the Written Word

Humans often consider the power of speech and written word to be the defining quality that sets us apart from the rest of the animal world. Although some animals have been trained through extensive teaching to communicate, Koko the Gorilla, for instance, humans alone possess the demonstrated ability for the use of language on an ongoing basis. Much like our Bio-Universal energy, we use language to hurt and we use it to help. That is why it is so much a part of Energy Magic.

There is little denying the power of words. For something used so carelessly, we do take them very seriously. We all have memories of times when words cut us to the bone and left us to bleed. Theory says it takes 100 positive words to make up for one negative one. Sometimes, words imprint on our psyches to the point that they become the filter through which we experience our lives. Words can damage our lives forever and the interesting part is that the person doing the wounding may have no idea they have hurt us or changed us in some significant way.

Likewise, hearing positive, uplifting words can bring our whole day into the sunlight. We thrive on hearing good things about ourselves and the experience can dramatically change our attitudes. Words can give us a completely new perspective when nothing else will do the job. Words are power.

Information is power and information is conveyed with words, written or spoken. It is a very pregnant moment when you know something that will change another person's life and you are about to make the big reveal. Think of the impact, positive or negative, of the following words and the circumstances in which you might have vastly different reactions to the exact same words:

*You're fired*

*I'm pregnant*

*Your husband is having an affair*

*Dad died last night*

*You look really fat in that dress*

*My friend thinks you are so hot*

*I can't stop thinking about you*

*I'm moving away*

*The job is yours if you want it*

*I do*

*I don't believe you can do that*

*The test was negative*

All of these phrases are only words and each has no power in and of itself. Again, like with intent, the designation of "bad" or "good" comes from within us. The words themselves convey only neutral information. Our own interpretation is what brings the power to the punch.

"I'm pregnant," for instance, can mean something different to a couple struggling for years with infertility than it does for a sixteen-year-old girl telling her mother the same exact words in the same configuration.

The news, "Barrack Obama has been elected president" is simply news. It is an objective fact that occurred. One of our friends went to bed for three days sobbing with the belief that our country was now doomed. Another of our friends had a three-day party to celebrate. Same news; different reactions created solely by their personal interpretations of that objective fact.

Magic is very deeply rooted in emotion. It is emotion that fuels most of our most motivations and desires. Beyond the basic drives of food, shelter, water, and air, nearly every other need is born of a particular emotion or cocktail of emotions. Since emotions are so much a part of our human motivations, it makes sense that they would be a big part of our magical construct.

Words have varying degrees of power depending on their delivery. The written word is very solid, substantial, and provable, but it lacks inflection, which is a big part of human communication. The advent of email as a primary form of communication has proven responsible for tremendous miscommunication simply because the receiver of the information is unable to read facial expression and voice tone. This was, of course, also a problem with actual hand-written letters; however, the use of written word for communication has increased astronomically since email became popular. The net result is that there are far more miscommunications due to lack of inflection than even ten years ago.

On the other hand, the spoken word is fleeting. "That's not what I said" has to be one of the most frequently used phrases known to humankind. Unless a conversation is tape recorded, words that are spoken are often twisted and misconstrued and not always maliciously! We hear and see through filters of conditioning that change how we interpret things people say to us. When we write a message, it is provable. The context and inflection is up for debate, but the words are there in black and white.

Thought is the most insubstantial form of wording. Our thoughts, to steal a metaphoric phrase, "tumble in our heads, making and breaking alliances like underpants in a tumble dryer." Our thoughts have power; do not get us wrong. Thoughts are the seeds from which all form manifests.

Once you turn your thoughts into words, spoken or written, their power increases tremendously. You may have heard the phrase, "You can't un-ring the bell." Once we speak something aloud, it cannot be unsaid. Hurtful words, for instance, can scar us deeply. The person who offended us can apologize with the most sincere, articulate, emotional apology imaginable and offer up all of the right reasons for why they said something so hurtful. We can forgive them, move on, and have a positive relationship with them. We will, however, always know that they can say hurtful, horrible things. We may convince ourselves that they will not do it again, but the knowledge that they are capable of doing so will never go away. That is the kind of irrevocable impact words have once they stop rattling around in your head and exit by way of mouth or pen.

Words have a hierarchy of impact in power. From least to greatest:

*1. Words that are still only thoughts*

*2. The spoken word*

*3. The written word*

*4. Written words that are spoken aloud*

*5. Written words that are spoken loud in front of others (witnesses)*

*6. Written words that are spoken aloud repeatedly (chanting or affirmations)*

Certainly, we can pray in our heads and we can work magic in our heads without saying a word. It is not a matter of such an act being impossible, but more that there is a greater impact when the words are spoken aloud.

Try this experiment:

*Think the words, "I am afraid. I am afraid. I am afraid."*

*Now say just the three words aloud and put as much meaning into them as you can.*

*"I am afraid."*

Can you feel the difference in impact? Even though you said the words three times in the first run and only once in the second run, the second time likely had greater impact for you.

This is why speaking our will aloud and in some cases, speaking it aloud repeatedly, accentuates the flow of energy toward a particular goal. As we say a phrase repeatedly, we naturally lend accent to different parts of the phase or sentence. This causes us to consider the phrase or sentence differently and internalize the information on a different level.

Journals have been an important part of thinking through and processing what goes on in our lives since people first put pen to paper. Lists bring organization to the world. Looking at words in print makes them more real and vital. Writing out your thoughts and then your intentions gives them tremendous substance. Contracts are binding and we feel that when we put promises, goals, and wishes into print. The words written by your own hand, in your own penmanship, are a very intimate and personal act.

This is why making a written account of your magical work and writing about your intention also gives it more power. Writing your name or other magical messages on the tools you use for your energy work also lends power.

Some people who work with esoteric energy enjoy using ancient languages. The Jewish faith uses the Hebrew language when they read the Torah and the Catholic faith uses Latin for some of their recitations. Most Christian Bible readings are in the nomenclature of the time in which they were written; not in our own way of speaking. Each of these spiritual paths assigns great power to the strength of the spoken and written word. Some magical paths appreciate the use of systems such as the Theban alphabet, Sanskrit, Aramaic, and Latin. This has its merit and there is a different type of power that is instilled into words that have been treated as holy and sacred by thousands and thousands of people over a long period of time. Amen, adonai, tetragrammaton, Yahweh, Ateh, Malkuth, Ve Geburah, Ve Gedullah, Le Olam… these are all holy words that have power amplified within them due to thousands of years of use as an esoteric and sacred language.

The issue with foreign language, regardless of how sacred it might be, is one of comprehension and focus. If the person using the words understands fully what they mean and use that meaning within their magical work, then the words become a process that help facilitate the flow of energy and even amplify it. If, however, the person is distracted by whether or not their pronunciation will be correct or if they do not know the true meaning and correct usage of the word and are only using it for flash and show, then it is likely to be a detriment to the successful flow of energy.

God loves an educated person who uses their knowledge artfully in communication. God does not appreciate a show off.

Just as there is tremendous power in the written word and the spoken word, there is also a specific energy in silence. The Wiccans have a lovely dictate called The Witch's Pyramid that goes like this:

To<br>Know<br>To Dare<br>To Will &<br>To Be Silent

This is a beautiful demonstration of the power of self-control. "To Know" means to know when to act and when to be still. "To Dare" means to be brave enough to act when it is necessary and not just worry a situation to death or doubt yourself into paralysis. "To will" means to have the conviction of truth and good intent and "make it so." "To Be Silent" means that once you have worked your Energy Magic, you do not talk it to death and bleed away all of the energy from the process. There are times when working quietly and keeping your own counsel is the best course of action.

Silence is a process that is not comfortable to most people in our society of constant stimulation and contact. Many people who are now grown do not remember at time when adults were not tethered to a cell phone and within constant access. It is common for people to have the television on when they are not even watching a program "for company." We reach out to one another through our computer and texting. It is rare that we are ever truly alone or completely out of reach of others and it is even less common for us to be alone *and in total silence.*

We are likely more "heard" now than in any other time in history. Not only do we communicate through normal channels, but also we now have message boards, blogs, and social networks to share our thoughts on an ongoing basis. We love these outlets as much as anyone, but we do feel that we have lost a true learning place when we use them exclusively and do not take advantage of times of silence and isolation. We do not always have to speak to be important. We do not always have to be on tap to others to be important. We are safe to listen to our own wisdom and inner voice rather than the stereo, radio, or television. An old saying regarding God is, *"In the silence, you will know me."* Removing the noise, bustle, and distraction from around us for a few minutes a day helps us to get in contact with our Higher Self on a more intimate level and therefore, access the Universal Energy more easily.

Runes and symbols are another form of communication and language that both the Higher Self and the Conscious Self understand. Using symbols and simple pictures speaks to both Selves simultaneously and helps them to coordinate their efforts. If we show the average person a simple picture of a sun:

...most people will have both their Higher Self and Conscious Self think of the thought of "sun" at the same time. Many symbols create a reaction in both selves and work to establish a simple language that bridges the gap between our two sacred personalities.

Runes are ancient glyphs that have certain meanings ascribed to them. The Germanic runes are the most often used:

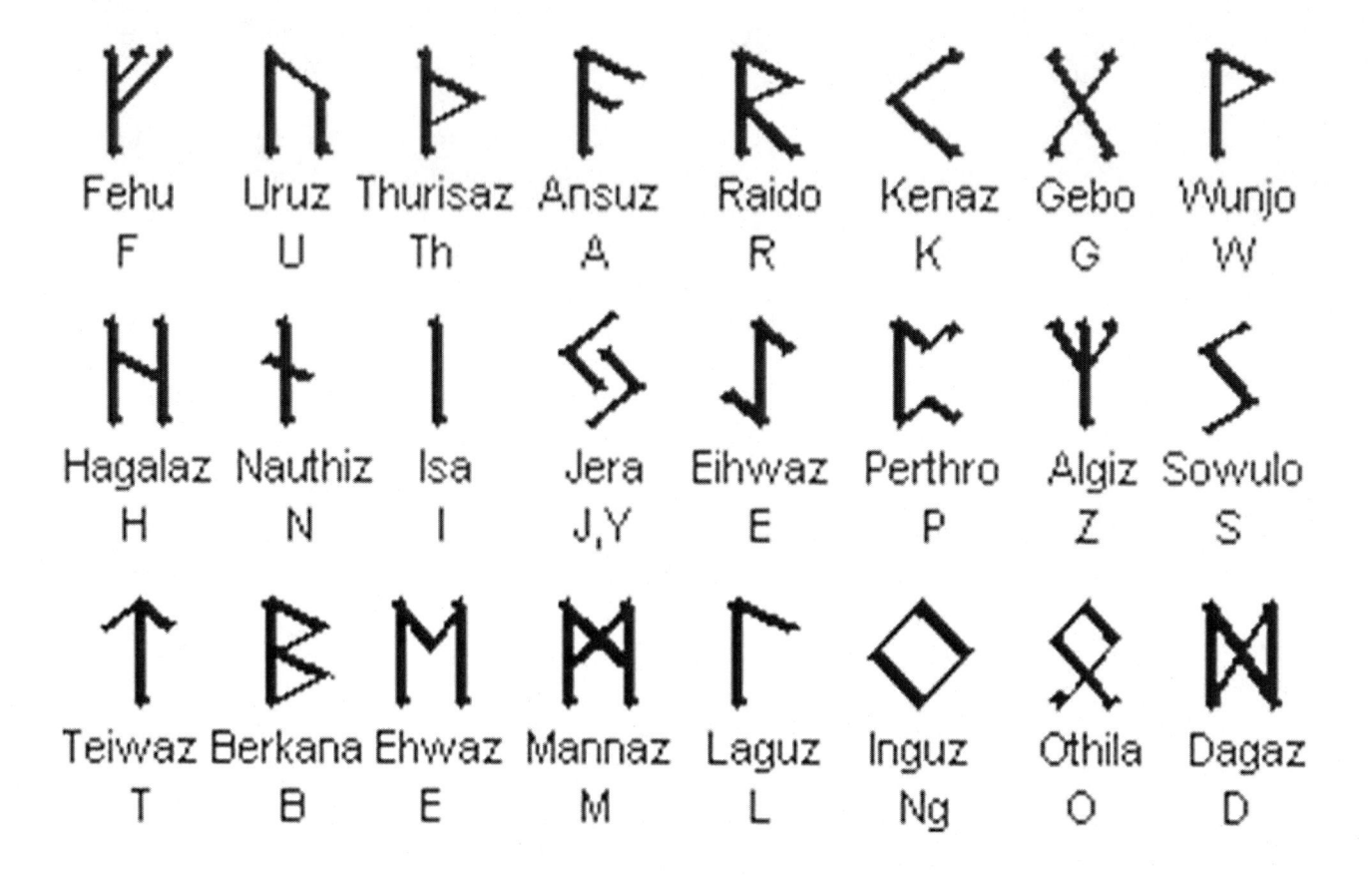

| Rune | Name | Letter |
|---|---|---|
| ᚠ | Fehu | F |
| ᚢ | Uruz | U |
| ᚦ | Thurisaz | Th |
| ᚨ | Ansuz | A |
| ᚱ | Raido | R |
| ᚲ | Kenaz | K |
| ᚷ | Gebo | G |
| ᚹ | Wunjo | W |
| ᚺ | Hagalaz | H |
| ᚾ | Nauthiz | N |
| ᛁ | Isa | I |
| ᛃ | Jera | J, Y |
| ᛇ | Eihwaz | E |
| ᛈ | Perthro | P |
| ᛉ | Algiz | Z |
| ᛊ | Sowulo | S |
| ᛏ | Teiwaz | T |
| ᛒ | Berkana | B |
| ᛖ | Ehwaz | E |
| ᛗ | Mannaz | M |
| ᛚ | Laguz | L |
| ᛜ | Inguz | Ng |
| ᛟ | Othila | O |
| ᛞ | Dagaz | D |

These are often engraved or drawn onto various magical tools and writings to add their energy to the work. Someone who wants to have a baby could use Inguz, the fertility rune. Alziz is a rune of protection if a person feels threatened in some way. Ehwaz is a rune of movement and can get things flowing if there has been a state of limbo or stagnation.

## Creating a Common Group Goal

There is absolutely no way to convey the impact of concerted group focus in a process of manifestation. Prayer chains the world over are dedicated specifically to the act of harnessing group energy and directing it toward a common goal. People gather for worship in churches and synagogues and circles to share the sacred experience and enhance the power of worship.

This effect is described in the world of physics by Sir Isaac Newton as "net force." We can push a car by ourselves and exert 25 Newtons (a measurement of force) to get the car moving. If a friend joins us and contributes 25 Newtons of force, the effort to move the car now has 50 Newtons of force behind it and will go twice as fast. The combination of your 25 Newtons and your friend's 25 Newtons is the "net force" that is pushing the car. If your archenemy shows up and pushes against the front of the car with the force of 10 Newtons, your net force is now 40 Newtons.

The same principle applies to the "force" you use to push your own Bio-Universal energy toward its goal. If you need money to pay your rent and you center up, pull up your own Bio-energy, connect in with God and feel the Universal energy flowing, mix them together into a happy energy cocktail, amplify them with some incense made with herbs and oils that are good for drawing in money, burn a green candle to bring in the focus of money and send your will out into the ether, you will likely get a good result. You combine the net force of all of those sympathetic energies toward your goal. Each tool you use contributes more force to the process.

So let's say that your own energy gave you 20 units of energy. Tapping into the God energy matched that and gave you another 20 units. Adding the color and herb boost gave you another 10 units. That means that instead of the 20 units you would have if you just wished for something to happen, you now have 50 units of force moving toward your goal.

If you get a friend to add their energy, you just got another 20K. Get three friends and you have another 60K of energy. The more people you add to the concentrated focus on your goal, the greater the flow of energy and the bigger the result. Group focus toward an Energy Magic goal is a tremendous asset to the process.

Can you do it on your own? Absolutely and without a doubt. If you can do it with a group, however, the results are much stronger.

## Astrological Influences & Timing

Assigned to them by people over the ages, the planets, the Moon, and the Sun have a particular energy to them. The Sun is strong, aggressive, and omnipresent. This caused people over time to think of it as a masculine energy. The moon is elusive, cyclic, and mysterious. These qualities caused people to think of it as feminine.

Mercury is considered the planet of the messenger because of its swift orbit around the sun. Venus is the planet of love. Earth is home: grounding and healing. Mars is the planet of war. Jupiter is the lively trickster. Saturn is the planet of limitations and lessons. Uranus is the planet of mystery and wisdom. Neptune represents change and adaptation.

In astrology, the Sun represents the foundation on which our personality is built. The planet that is coming over the horizon at the minute we are born is called the ascendant or the rising sign. The ascendant is the house we build on the foundation the Sun provides and it is what people usually see of our personality. The Moon is the interior of our soul that we use to furnish the house and is the innermost part of ourselves that only a few will see.

The Sun moves through 12 signs in a year's time. They each have their own energy to lend. The moon moves through those same signs as well, in addition to the phases of New (Dark Moon), Full, Waxing, and Waning.

All of these contribute energy toward what we do every day and they certainly can be a tremendous asset to our energy flow if we learn how they influence our daily life.

The phase of the moon, for instance, lends the energy of the cycle of new beginnings and fruition. The New Moon period is a time of growth and fresh starts. Waxing Moon is a good time to begin actions and work toward adding to your life in some way. Full Moon is a time of fruition and fullness. Waning Moon is a time to work toward what you would like to have leave your life and diminish.

We can phrase nearly all goals in such a way as to use the energy of the moon phase in which we are working. For instance, if a person's goal is to lose weight, they might be stymied if it is a New Moon. New Moons are for gaining, not for losing! They can, however, ask for will power, good health, a strong and vibrant body, greater self-esteem, etc. Working for wealth and prosperity to grow can be shifted to banishing poverty and want. Just turn your wishes inside out to fit the Moon cycle!

The energy of other astrological forces is available to accentuate your efforts by nature of their characteristics. Aries is a very assertive sign. Taurus loves creature comforts. Virgo is very organized. Gemini thinks quickly. Learn the positive qualities of the Sun and Moon sign in which you are working and call on their influence to accentuate your magical work.

## Stones

People often laugh at "New Agers" for using quartz crystals as focus tools. If you hold quartz in your hand and focus your energy through it, the quartz regulates the flow of energy through your body. If you hold the crystal correctly, it regulates the flow of energy *out* of your body and toward a goal. That is why wands, tools used to project your energy toward a certain target, often have quartz crystal at the far end. That may sound silly until you consider that very tiny quartz crystals are used to regulate the energy of what? *Watches.* Watches are some of the most intricate constructions ever invented by humankind and a tiny crystal regulates the pulses of energy inside it. It is less silly when you imagine that the same quartz crystal that can regulate pulses of energy inside a watch can regulate the pulses of energy in and from your body.

Hematite is a silvery, shiny, magnetic stone. Named as it is for its ability to pull impurities out of the bloodstream, it can discharge negative energy out of the body or out of a situation.

As we quoted earlier in this text, *"There are more things in heaven and earth, Horatio, than are dreamt of in your philosophy."* There is such an abundance of things on this earth that we do not understand. Fortunately, it is exciting to have so many fresh frontiers yet to explore and it is fortunate as well that we do not *have* to understand to gain the benefits. God exists in all things, all through nature, and this being the case, the energy that is inherent in stones, herbs, and other natural structures. The bits of energy living in these items, waiting to release, are like special gifts from God to boost our personal energy.

In our appendices, you will find a list of the properties of different stones. You can put stones with the qualities you wish to invoke out on your hearth or your dresser, you can carry them in your pocket or against your body. You can even put them into a little mojo bag with other items that are sympathetic to your goals (items you consider sacred, herbs that help your cause, etc) and carry or wear the bag.

## Weather

Of all of the factors we could discuss that amp up magical energy, for both of us, there is nothing like a rainstorm. From the smell of those first few drops hitting parched land to the thunder and lightning all the way through the rivers of water running down the road, rain wakes up our Higher Selves in a big way. A friend of ours is terrified of thunderstorms and tries to sleep until they are over. We are the ones running out into the middle of typhoons (literally) and electrical storms and hurricanes trying to tap that natural energy and feel it course all through us. We feel the power of Nature and God in those moments.

A warm spring day is magical with the earth softening from the grip of winter, a soft breeze carrying the scent of daffodils and the promise of new beginnings. Eric feels most alive with the sun beating down hard on him in the summer days, relaxing on his boat with the lake breeze in his face.

We all have our special metrological times and should take full advantage of them when they occur. Sensory experiences that we can see, smell, hear, feel, and taste are some of the strongest motivators of magical energy. When the weather that you love comes around, use your appreciation of it to fuel your magical efforts.

## Visual Cues

Humans respond very strongly, sometimes at a visceral and subconscious level, to what they see in front of them. When a Catholic person prays the Rosary, they use the beads as a focus tool that they can see and touch as they pray. When a person misses someone they love, they will often hold an article of clothing that smells like the person they miss and acts as a visual reminder of a time when they were not apart. We keep photos of our loved ones on our walls and our mantles and in our wallets to evoke a feeling when we see them.

What we see around us is extremely instrumental in determining our mood and the energy we will emit. In order to live the sacred life full time, truly living the ordinary life in an extraordinary way, beautiful, sacred items that awaken the magical energy inside of us and stimulate our Higher Selves to come into stronger presence should surround us. This does not have to be an expensive endeavor. Sometimes, it is as simple as bringing in fresh flowers from outside, moving our furniture around, and creating a different kind of energy flow in our home.

There are many techniques for creating harmonious energy around us. Honoring the four natural elements in each room is a good start. Create a special place for earth, air, fire, and water in your rooms. Again, this does not have to be elaborate. A shell can suffice for water, a stone for earth, a feather for air, and a candle for fire. If you live at the end of a street that results in cars constantly moving toward your home, then turning, put a small mirror (compact size mirror or smaller) on the ground against your house so that it points toward the cars. Make sure it does not blind anyone if sunlight hits it. It can have grass or bushes in front of it. The idea is to reflect the constant flow of erratic energy back the way it came so that it does not over-stimulate your house. Many books are available about creating a magical home. Most notable is Scott Cunningham's, *The Magical Household.*

Haunt thrift stores, yard sales, and second hand shops for statues and paintings that awaken your spirit and send it soaring into the stars. Never be afraid to nurture yourself in this way. The more you work to create a sacred environment around you all of the time, the more connected, fulfilled, and happy you will be. This in turn will cause you to radiate joy, Bio-Universal energy, and light. Really, nourishing your aesthetic delights is a service to those around you, assisting you in showing them your very best self.

It is hard to cultivate a holy and sacred vibe in a room or house that is disorderly, dirty, and full of stale air. (You know what to do).

Visual cues are very important for pulling your focus onto the target in your magical work. Wish board and goal boards are a lovely way to amplify your energy toward a goal. Pictures of your goal fulfilled and representations of where you want to be when the process is over are also powerful tools.

If your magical energy is directed to a person for protection, healing, or other work, a photo of the person is a nice point of focus. You can light candles around the picture or highlight it in some other way. Some people like to personalize their energy work with their own tears, blood (menstrual blood is very effective), fingernails, hair, or other DNA bits, and other points of focus. Anything that assists you in feeling connected to the work you are doing and amplifies the energy you are able to generate toward that work is a great addition.

# Chapter 8 - Properties of Energy – What Slows It Down?

If we go back to the idea of Newton's laws of physics, we know that friction is what resists motion. The law of inertia says that once an object is in motion, it will stay in motion until a force acts upon it and slows it down or stops it. This applies to energy as well. Energy continues until something slows it down or stops it. What we want, of course, is for our energy to move swiftly toward our goal with the strongest charge possible, free of obstacles or resistance. We have just explored some of the forces that can speed up our Energy Magic, but what slows it down or grounds it? What causes Energy Magic to "fail" or take longer?

It is very true that not every prayer is answered and not every ritual is successful in terms of the intentions the person had at the time it was enacted. If we know what can ground our energy and interfere with the connection, so to speak, we can sometimes avoid those pitfalls.

## The Influence of Fate/Greatest Good

As we have taught Energy Magic classes over the past years, we have many students ask us about the influence of Fate and Greatest Good on our proactive praying. What happens when God/The Universe/Goddess says, "No?" We cannot begin to count the number of earnest spells and prayers we have sent out with tremendously pure intent only to have them never bring about the manifestation we sought.

The other side of this is that every single time we did not get what we wanted, we got something better. In our arrogance, we assume we know exactly what is best for our lives and will sometimes even beg, plead, and wrestle with God over our own greatest good. This specifically will slow down positive results. It is a similar experience as a good parent who has a child who is throwing a tantrum because they cannot have or do what they want. The child wants to eat a huge bag of candy all at once or play in the street or go to the party with no adults present and the parent says, "No, that's not going to happen." The child does not have the experience, maturity, or long-term vision to understand why the parent is stopping the happy parade. All the child knows is that they can't have what they want and they're angry. In retrospect, with the benefit of greater knowledge, wisdom, and the passage of time, they are able better understand why it was a bad idea to fly off the roof pretending to be Superman.

As rational, reasonable adults, we make choices for our lives based on what we know at the time to be true. Our vision, however, is limited to our previous experiences and what we can see before us and around us at any given time. This Higher Power we call God, however, can see where we need to be for our own greatest good and works to direct us there. Most of our prayers and concerted Energy Magic work do not take us off track from that ultimate divine purpose. Some, however, would cause an unnecessary diversion that will delay or greatly limit our progress. Some could even take us into dangerous situations. These are the plans God will actively thwart.

Imagine that you are a warrior on the battlefield, swinging the sword in the midst of a raging war. All you know is the danger that is before you and behind you and all around you. You are tired and sore and pumped full of adrenalin. You are fighting for your life, so your job is to stay alert, swing that sword, and block with that shield. The King, however, is on a horse on a hilltop overlooking the valley where you are fighting. The king can see the entire battlefield, including what is sneaking up from the woods behind you, the weather that is coming over the horizon, and the additional, fresh troops that are closing in from the South to assist. We do not have the panoramic view to see what is coming to help or hurt us, but God, like that King, can see beyond what we know.

In early 1996, Katrina did some Energy Magic to create joy in her life. She went to her son's high school production of *The Sound of Music* and the opening act was a dance troupe called "The Swing Kids." These were high school kids who performed swing dancing and while they danced, each one had a big, beaming smile. The thing was, the smiles did not look like stage props. They were genuine. The kids were having a blast. As she watched them with the uncomfortable bleachers of the gymnasium digging into her butt, she realized that she had no idea how that felt. She had never really felt that kind of joy before and she wanted some. Later that night, she did some spell work to welcome joy into her life and to ask the Goddess to help her to find her way to true joy.

The next day, it was business as usual, but a few short weeks later, her husband at that time told her very unexpectedly that he was in love with someone else and that a divorce was not negotiable. She was completely blind-sided and devastated. He and she had previously divorced and remarried. She loved him with all her heart and had no indication that he was unhappy or did not want to be with her prior to his announcement She dragged him through counseling, but all the counselor did was to try and prepare her for the inevitable rather than heal the marriage. Her husband was already gone and it was just a matter of his body and possessions following suit.

She prayed. She begged. She cried. She beat on the ground. She cursed the Goddess. She was so furious not only to have been betrayed as she was, but to be put in the same situation all over again after all the promises and rebuilding and reinvested trust. She had no more hopes or dreams left because every hope and dream she could imagine connected directly to him. On top of it all, he was leaving her for a *really, really homely woman.* All of her Energy Magic focused on him returning to the home, living up to his promises, and repairing their family. This is where the power of free will stops Energy Magic in its tracks. Her husband's desire to leave was far more powerful than her energy work to get him to stay. Was her work unethical? Absolutely. One should never do energy work that conflicts with the free will of another. Emotional upheaval and fatigue can cause anyone to shift their principles in desperation. Fortunately, as you can see, there is a stop-gap measure that causes this sort of energy expenditure to ground and neutralize. Staying with her husband was NOT in her best interest and the Universe decided it was time for them both to move on.

Finally, she started to understand the message that he was going to leave, her marriage was over, she could do nothing to stop it. For a while, she thought if she could only find the right words, he would change his mind. Eventually, she began to prepare for her life as a single mom yet again. It was one of the most horrible experiences she had ever known and it took her months of resisting to finally let go and allow the current of the raging river to carry her to whatever destiny the Universe had in mind for her.

A few months later, she met Eric, her current husband and co-author of this book. She told herself it was too soon, he was too young (he is fifteen years younger), and a few hundred other reasons why she should not be completely captivated by this man. A year later, they were married, just two weeks before her ex-husband married the other woman.

A few years later, she finally connected the destruction and pain associated with the most recent divorce to the energy work she had done to bring joy to her life. God was wiser than she was and knew that she could not experience true joy in the relationship she had at that time, in the location where she was, doing what she was doing. She asked for joy and in order to get it, her entire life had to blow up and she had to suffer through the most pain she had ever known. She did, however, get the joy and went on to embrace her own greatest good, which ended up nothing like she thought it was supposed to be. It was so much better. It took years for that joy to take hold, but big things like that take time. Now, she lives a completely joyful life. She has a good friendship with her first husband and her current husband is invested in giving her a wonderful life.

In this particular instance, she did not know what was best for her. She was certain that she did and she worked the most intensive magic she could manage but none of it was effective. Her magic was very specific: let her keep her marriage. She bartered and begged and threatened and nothing worked. No amount of energy investment or magic was going to manifest her goal *because it was not in her best interest or for her greatest good*. In fact, she could never fulfill her life's mission if things did not change right away.

This is an excellent example of a very important lesson, which is that if your magic is not taking hold, it is time to "let go and let God." Something is going on that is bigger than what you know and the best thing to do is to take your hands off of it and *trust the process*. When you stop fighting your inevitable trip down the rapids toward your own greatest good and instead, relax and enjoy the ride with the complete faith that *God will take care of you*. You will get there faster and without the damage you will sustain from resisting. As the old song says, *"Be not dismayed what e'er betide. God will take care of you."* Sometimes, what you want *is just not meant to be* and it is not meant to be purely for your own protection and ultimate fulfillment. When you trust that one premise, you have mastered the process. As with Katrina's experience, when you let go of what you think you want, what you truly want will appear. Over time, this surrender becomes left frightening and more empowering.

If your Energy Magic does not divert you from the higher purpose of your life, then it will likely take hold if your intent is pure and you connect in on a strong level. If you are working for a condition that will take you away from your higher life purpose and interfere with what will ultimately bring you satisfaction and joy, then it is likely your energy will ground and neutralize.

When you work toward a goal using Energy Magic and begin to encounter resistance to that process, the first thing you have to ask yourself is, *"Is this a redirect to tell me that I need to revamp my goal or create a new one or is it a challenge to test how much I want this?"* The vast majority of the time, it is a message that you need to reframe your goal or focus on it in a different way.

For instance, let's say that you are losing your home and you want to work to save it. You do not want to move because you love your house and it would be a tremendous effort to relocate. Your Energy Magic efforts are centered on staying in your home, but external circumstances are not coming together to support that goal and there is no reprieve in sight. How do you reframe? It is time to work toward *the way you want to feel* because of your Energy Magic efforts. What you want to *feel* is that you have a safe, attractive, special home that is perfect for your needs and that you have the means to afford it. Rather than focus so much energy on this one home, even if you have excellent reasons to stay there, open your mind to the idea that life may take you elsewhere, but ultimately, it will be for your greatest good.

Ego demands that we hold fast to our idea of how things should be and believe that we know best. It is a tremendous act of faith to surrender our control over to The Universe and allow things to unfold as they will. This act of surrender, however, is a tremendous tool in Energy Magic. We do not have to control every little moment and sometimes, the highest and best course of action is to let go and allow the world to turn a few more times to let the situation develop. There are likely influences and bits of information that we do not yet have that we must wait to learn. Pushing for our own wants all the time is not the way to go. We have to allow for the influence of Fate and Greatest Good to intertwine with our own intention to create the most positive outcome. That is specifically the gift of Energy Magic: the blending of Bio and Universal energies into the most rewarding life we can possibly live.

## The Influence of Free Will

In the various Pagan paths, it is a standard ethic that you never ask The Universe for something that affects another person's free will. For instance, you do not ask the Universe to "make" someone love you if he or she does not have those feelings. You do not ask that someone to leave their home or job if you know that is not their desire. This is practical as well as ethical because the power of a person's free will is very strong. It takes a tremendous amount of personal energy to manipulate another person's life and usually, such manipulation is NOT in our own greatest good anyway and will likely ground and neutralize as it did with Katrina. The point of Energy Magic is to work on yourself and your own life, not someone else's.

As with the Moon phases, however, there are ways to work around the free will aspect and still get what you want. Considering the idea of "making" someone love us, we have to think about the fact that even if that happened, some part of us would always know that they do not love us for us and who we truly are, but because they were influenced by the energy. What we are asking for in this case is a particular feeling and a particular relationship as opposed to a certain person. We may *think* it can only come through that one person, but the true issue is a way we want to feel inside. Remember that all magic comes first from a feeling.

In this case, it is best to focus on that feeling and work on drawing it in without any assignment to a particular person for that fulfillment. We write a list of the qualities we seek in a relationship (remember the power of the written word) and read it aloud to ourselves (power of the spoken word). This fulfills our goal without affecting the free will of another. It is possible that if the person we are attracted to actually does have feelings for us, the Energy Magic will wake them up and bring them to the surface. That is *not* interfering with free will but merely calling attention to something that is already there.

If there is someone in your life who you would really like to see gone, a good way to manage that with Energy Magic is to draw in a happy reason for them to leave. If the person is at your place of work, imagine that they get a promotion or a better job and leave to pursue that opportunity. If the person is at your home or in your circle of friends, imagine that their heart's desire takes them to a better location. This way, they have the option to accept what comes to them or not, so no free will issues are created.

One of the fastest ways that Energy Magic grounds and neutralizes is by your own free will getting in the way. Let's say you don't have a job and you know you really need one and if you don't get one, you're going to be in a serious financial lurch. You work Energy Magic to get a job, but a part of you really wants to stay home in bed and not go to work. If your entire will is not behind the energy you send to your goal, your overall force will be divided and weakened. It is important that you do the homework, so to speak, and clear away any internal obstacles you may have to your success. Maybe you ask that a relationship be healed when that really is not what you want. You might ask to attract buyers to your house when you really do not want to move. Free will choices will not always derail your Energy Magic, but it can most certainly slow it down.

Another way that free will has a major impact on magical endeavors is in the practice of gambling. One would think it would be easy to go to a slot machine, roulette wheel, or a card table send some energy toward the cards or the wheel and pour out a jackpot. The problem with gambling (including lotteries) is that you are placing your free will choices up against those of many others who all want the target just as much as you do. The free will of all of those people pulls against and balances out your own free will interests. The free will desires of the casino are also at play. In short, gambling is one of the very few completely neutral places where if it is meant to be, it will be.

## Lack of Cohesion

God is very forgiving and knows your heart before you speak your will. Your "presentation" of your intention, goal, and wish is merely to amplify your own part of the energy boost. In the previous section, we talked about the importance of making sure that your entire being is behind the intention you put forward rather than some part of yourself pulling in a different direction. Energy Magic flows best when your intent is clear and focused and your environment is supportive and calm.

If you get your ritual area all set up and believe that you are ready to go and things start to fall apart, it is time to pay attention. You light your correctly colored candles and the dog knocks over a plant in the next room. You center up and prepare to court your Higher Self and your child, who you thought was sleeping, wakes up and needs attention. You come back to find that your candles went out and you have to relight them. After you get the candles lit, someone knocks at the door… and so it goes.

During those inevitable times when you find that despite your best efforts, your ritual seems to be falling apart around you, it is critical that you stop and recognize what is happening rather than continuing to "herd the cats." If one or two things trip you up, that is not normally cause for concern. If you experience a greater number of interfering factors, then it is time to get the message. Usually, this is The Universe telling us that it is not yet time for us to do the Energy Magic we were about to enact. *Why?*

> *It was inappropriate for reasons we do not yet know (or we do know and we are ignoring).*
>
> *We need more information before proceeding*
>
> *The ritual itself needs to be re-thought and re-framed. Something is off.*
>
> *Energies are already in motion toward your goal and no further work is necessary. (Usually, this will not slow you down, but I have known it to happen)*

As humans, we very much want to believe that we know what is best at any given time and often cannot imagine that we may not have the full picture. Humility and grace are valuable tools in Energy Magic. It is helpful to heed the gentle nudges from the Universe. These help us to tune into the flow of natural progression with a much cleaner and stronger signal.

If you choose to continue with your Energy Magic ritual despite The Universe's attempt to curtail your work, it is not likely that you will bring about Armageddon. It is more likely that your energy will be ground and neutralize or you will not obtain optimal results. Overall, it is better to stop what you are doing, wait a few hours while you re-evaluate your approach, then try again from a different angle at a different time. Almost always, the reason for the delay or change becomes clear as time goes on.

## Physical Discomfort/Illness

Distraction is one of the fastest ways for your energy to lose speed and you will notice that many of our detriments to good energy flow have an element of distraction to them. Focus is important and the more of your attention you can commit to the Energy Magic process, the better your results will be.

Physical discomfort is a tremendous distraction and can have quite an impact on your ability to focus. In church, some people find hard pews and kneeling stools to be uncomfortable. In Pagan circles, working outside is often far, far too cold in the later months. Headaches, cramps, sinus problems and other maladies can all work to rob you of precious focus and energy. When most people are ill, their body energies focus naturally on the healing process and energy reserves that are normally available for Energy Magic use are otherwise engaged. It takes even more energy to pull them away from the healing they are attempting to facilitate and go outward into a magical direction.

It is hard to feel magical if your feet are stinging from being cold or you are sweltering and can feel your skin burning in the sun. Making certain that you are as physically comfortable as possible is a big part of protecting your energy resources for ritual time to achieve optimum energy output.

Sometimes, unexpected physical discomfort such as a headache, stomach cramps, or other temporary illnesses are signs of the cat herding analogy, telling you that this magical act needs to wait until another time.

Another aspect of physical comfort is fatigue. Fatigue affects not only our physical energy level, but also rational thought and our ability to focus. Sleep deprivation is, in fact, a tactic of torture used on prisoners of war! Working effective magic when you are sleep-compromised and exhausted is almost impossible.

Make certain that you are rested, centered, and physically comfortable when it comes time to work your Energy Magic.

## High Emotion/Hormonal Shifts

Emotion is a big part of what fuels Energy Magic because it is at the heart of *what you want to have happen*. If you cannot feel, then you cannot want. High emotion of all kinds: love, fear, sadness, anger, frustration, etc, can definitely fuel your energy like a stoked furnace.

On the other hand, high emotion can also occasionally render us unreasonable and irrational. It is completely up to the person to determine whether they are in a mentally stable place to approach an Energy Magic task. The biggest question regarding high emotion is motivation and intent. If you are using Energy Magic to create a positive outcome for yourself or others, then that is a pure intent. If you are using your energy to get revenge on someone else, that is not a good time to go into ritual.

Hormonal shifts can play with our emotions and cause us to have unbalanced reactions to situations. This is true for both males and females. It is best to go into an Energy Magic ritual with a level head, but full of strong intent fueled by positive emotion. That positive emotion can take the form of "hope" if the current situation is challenging. Certainly, to work Energy Magic, you do not have to live in a world of rainbows, puppy dogs, and roses. You should make sure, however, that when you go into ritual, you are pure of intent and thinking clearly.

Many of us have had those moments when we go into ritual, crying the ugly cry and full of rage, appealing to our favorite goddess, *"I…want…you…to…KILL HIM!"* Many people go into prayer filled with righteous indignation over a wrong done to them. OK, maybe not everyone has had this experience, but we are willing to bet more than a few have! (*Katrina: "Shhh, I have! But don't tell anyone!"*)

When we are full of emotion to the point that we cannot make good choices, it is like drunk dialing God. *Not a good plan.* If there is a case where you are wronged in some way and feel the need to work Energy Magic to right the wrong, the best course of action is to put up protection around you and those you love and leave the rest until another day when you are more focused. If you want to know more about protecting yourself, check out our book called *Magical Ethics and Protection* to stay on the ride side of the Karma bus (instead of in front of it).

## Bad Vibes

Another form of discomfort that can distract you from good magical focus is just plain old bad vibes. This can have to do with a general feeling of unease or emotional/psychic discomfort. It can also due to someone in the immediate area with whom you have a complicated or contentious relationship. Other times, it can be because of the area in which you are working is charged with negative energy from a recent experience.

If you are in a ritual with other people and you begin to get the heebie jeebies and feel uncomfortable, above all *trust yourself*. It is time for you to leave. You should never stand there and try and talk yourself into staying or doubt your own impulses. Go! Proper etiquette is to ask someone in charge to "cut a door" for you in the energy so that you may leave without disturbing everyone else. If you are refused the right to leave, then you were right to be concerned and should leave immediately, with or without permission.

Under the best of situations, if you are uncomfortable in someone else's ritual, even if nothing hinky is going on, you will contaminate their magical process with your own discomfort, so it is always best to leave.

The same goes for any other religious ceremony. Over the past thirty years, we have probably walked out of every form of religious expression on earth at one time of another for our own comfort level. It is more respectful to leave than to remain and be uneasy. Even if the energy generated by the ceremony is only uncomfortable *to you*, it is best to leave than to remain and contaminate the experience with your own discomfort.

If you are working alone and become uncomfortable, you may need to "smudge" the area with incense or burning sage. This will remove negativity and create a cleaner and more psychically hospital area for you to use for Energy Magic work. It is customary for this to be part of your procedure for prepping the ritual area. Some people do not bother if they are very familiar with what has been in the area over the past several hours and feel there is no discord around.

Even if you have previously smudged, it never hurts to smudge again if you find that you are uncomfortable. This can also be another way that The Universe tells us to delay the process until another time. As before, follow your instinct and listen to the guidance you are given.

If you find yourself at a public gathering and see that someone is there with whom you have discord, it is respectful to the hosts to NOT enter into the ritual area unless you are certain you can purge away absolutely *all* negative thoughts and emotions and enter into the ritual area as a clean vessel, ready to work. It is not YOUR responsibility to concern yourself with how the other person feels or behaves. It is for you to manage your OWN energy in public.

Some Native American tribes had the custom of putting a lidded basket outside of their teepees. This was a "worry basket" and served as a visual reminder that one should not bring their troubles into the home of another. The idea was that you would put your worries into the basket as you went into the home and would take them with you again when you left.

For many years, we had a worry basket at the entrance to our magical working area to remind anyone who entered to leave his or her worries, drama, and fear behind and enter into the circle area with a clean spirit. One difference is that we encouraged people to LEAVE their problems in the basket and then after everyone left, we would cleanse the energy and dedicate it to the positive resolution of the problems that were left there.

## Smells

You know, it sounds simple. It is not. It can be a major distraction and energy drain if the area where you are working stinks...literally. A common smell that hosts may not notice they have is animal odors. People who live in an area with animals become habituated to the smells of their pets, but the smells of dogs, cats, snakes, or rodents can be overwhelming to guests. We have been in rituals where the smell of a cat box was so overpowering that our eyes burned. To say we were distracted and had difficulty focusing on the magical work at hand is quite an understatement. Odors are not limited to animals. Tobacco smells, trash, body odor, and spoiled food can be just as distracting.

This is not to say that you have to Lysol your entire house before you perform Energy Magic work, but it is important that all of your senses are comfortable and that distractions are minimized. As we have discussed, one of the greatest detriments to energy flow is distraction and it really is not that difficult to streamline your environment so that you do not have permeating influences that will pull you off task and reduce your energy flow.

## Psychic Vampires/Black Holes

We are sure that you have had experiences where you walk away from spending time with someone, even someone you like, and just felt drained. Some people are exhausting. Some people are needy and just pull the energy right out of you. Some people are contentious and argumentative and even someone who loves a good debate can grow tired of it after a while. Psychic vampires suck away your energy, which leaves less for you to direct toward your goal. It can be difficult to avoid those people who are energy black holes if they are in your family or work environment. We strongly advise that if you are going to do Energy Magic work, you should stay clear of these kinds of people for several hours before you work. You need your energy for *you* and the work you are doing. You should not pour it away unnecessarily. As you progress in living the magical life, you will see the benefit to distancing yourself entirely from those people who bleed the energy right out of you. You can love them, but not spend enough time with them that they tap out your energy resources.

## Clutter, Chatter, Chaos

You absolutely do not have to be a neat freak to work effective Energy Magic. Your environment does not have to be sterile and squeaky clean. It does help, however, to have an area that is free of clutter and chaos. Our minds register everything we see in our immediate environment. When we are working Energy Magic, ideally everything we see would make us feel empowered and magical. If our eyes have to see piles and piles of clutter and stuff everywhere, it is harder for the magical items to pop and register in our minds. All we see is "stuff."

If there is no place in your house that is clutter-free, your magical working area should at least be nicely organized and attractive. Your mind should be able to focus on the task at hand; not forty or fifty other things that need to be done. Clutter distracts our minds and pulls our focus away from the energy we direct.

Ritual does not have to be a solemn event by any means. Smiles and warmth are an important part of those feelings that fuel the energy. A nonstop gabfest however, can distract people from the intent of the moment. Words used should be at a minimum and pertain to the purpose of the ritual. There is plenty of time for socializing afterward.

## Geographical Area

Mountains, city, desert, rural country, grassy meadows, beaches… what is your calling? Different people react in different ways to the incredible variety our world offers in terms of landscape. Some people feel closest to the Goddess at the ocean with the spray on their faces and the warm surf at their feet. Others prefer the deep woods or warm desert. What calls to you? Usually, if you are in a geographical environment that is the direct opposite of your ideal location, your energy will not be as strong. For Katrina, for instance, the second she tries to work in a desert area, her energy output decreases significantly. We believe it is because she equates magical flow with water, which is scarce in the desert.

For many mundane reasons, people often do not live in their desired location and this section is not to discourage anyone from using Energy Magic if they are not in a climate or terrain that makes them feel magical. It is simply saying that if you do live in an area that you consider inhospitable to magical work, you may have to take extra care to protect and amplify your energy in other ways.

## Metal Jewelry

Metal is a material that holds energy very well. Many people we know have reacted to buying used jewelry, feeling there was bad energy stored in it. There are many simple processes to cleanse out metal objects and clear away any negative energy. Some people, however, find that different metals ground their energy. We have known folks who had to remove all rings, earrings, and bracelets before they worked in order to achieve the maximum energy push. Experiment and see if you are sensitive to metals in terms of your energy generating abilities. Some jewelry, particularly those with precious stones, can actually amp your energy instead of grounding it.

Metal, by nature, is a super conductor of energy and so in theory, it should amplify, not ground your energy. If you find that you are sensitive, see if it is to all metal or just particular types. There may be energies inherent in those items that are at work tapping out your own personal energy. It is a very interesting course of study and can assist you in managing your energy levels mundanely as well as magically.

# Worry/Lack of Faith

Over the years, we have had many students contact us saying that they worked magic for a specific outcome and now they wonder if they should do more magic to give it a boost. What they are saying is that they have not yet seen evidence that their magic is working and they are questioning whether they did the magic correctly or had enough energy to make it fly. They doubt themselves or they doubt that God heard and will reply. Either one is a dangerous path to follow. Some magical efforts are intentionally set up to be enacted over multiple sessions. If you want a "wave" effect that boosts the energy over a time, you can certainly set up your magic to work that way. This practice, however, is *not* a matter of questioning or doubting the process you followed. Worrying about the work you did and thinking you need to boost it because you do not yet see results *is*.

As we have mentioned before, The Universe knows your heart and intention before you speak it or work magic toward it. The work we do is to honor the Universal energies and to amplify our own personal energy to invest toward the goal. If you did it, you did it right. (period) Worry is nothing more than a lack of trust in "the process." It is saying that God does not know enough to keep you on the path toward your greatest good and create a positive outcome. Once you have engaged the Bio-Universal energies in an act of magic toward a specific goal, the most productive step you can take is to walk away from it knowing it was a job well done. If it does not bear fruit, then you must believe that for whatever reason, it was not meant to be *or was not meant to be right now*.

If you planted a seed, you would not go back a couple of weeks later and dig it up to see if it is growing. To do so would kill the very process you are trying to cultivate. Instead, you nourish it and wait patiently for signs of life. In magic, you do the same. Plant you seed and have faith that it will flourish into a garden of success and greatest good. That is the truest nature of putting your trust in The Universe. Make your will known, put your energy toward it, and then have the courage, conviction, and faith to walk away confident that it will be accomplished if it is for the greatest good.

## Harms None

This specific directive is common in the Pagan faiths, but is not included in the Christian faiths as a specific commandment. At first blush, it seems extremely loose and free compared to other spiritual mandates. You can do anything you want as long as you do not harm anyone.

What you have to consider, however, is that "harming" someone is a multi-level concept. It premises the idea that harm can occur on all five levels of existence: physical, emotional, sexual, mental, and spiritual. In our interactive society, we could include "social." We may not bring physical harm to someone, but could destroy a reputation with a few words or a careless accusation. We can say things to a child that have long lasting emotional repercussions for the child, but then forget that we said it an hour later. We can participate in an unhealthy dynamic long after we recognize that it is toxic because continuing the relationship the way it is brings us tremendous benefit, even if it is at the expense of another.

All of these actions are common in everyday life, even among "good" people. This is only considering human-to-human interaction. A whole other barrel of (possibly harmed) worms opens when we think about human-to-animal treatment. "Harm none" are two very power packed words that we should not take lightly, in ritual and out of it.

Sadly, harm on some level is almost inevitable if we believe in the 3rd law of Newtonian physics: *For every action, there is an equal and opposite reaction.* If we work to get a particular job, someone else does not get the job and possibly, it is someone who needs it worse than we do. If we work to create an opening in a long line of traffic to allow us to merge, several other people must change their driving to accommodate our space.

Whenever we work to bring something about, it affects the lives of others on some level, even in an extremely negligible way. If you slow down to allow another person to merge onto a crowded freeway, it likely has very little impact on you. If you are driving a laboring woman to the hospital and two or three people come flying off the on ramp and cut you off, you likely have a different reaction.

"Harms none" is not a fully realistic mandate. You are going to occasionally step on a bug or accidentally have 14 items on a 12 or fewer check out. While "harms none" is a mindset one should embrace to work Energy Magic effectively and ethically, it is also an ideal to which we aspire. It reminds us that what we do has an impact, big or small or in between or all through the spectrum. We should definitely give the ripple effect consideration in Energy Magic.

Why is this included in the "what slows energy down" section? Simply because of the other, not so incidental side of "harm none." We covered high emotions previously in this section and that idea ties in a bit to this one. The guidance with "harms none" is that we should never work magic that we know will deliberately harm another. You may work magic to put before them a free will choice that they may then accept or reject (a job in a different state, for instance, or a new home or a new partner). That then leaves the decision to them and is purely and safely within ethical boundaries.

You can protect yourself, your children, and other vulnerable loved ones from harm by putting up magical shields around you and them and/or doing a type of magic described later in this book called "reflect and return." It is, however, on very shaky grounds to attack someone magically, even if you feel he or she may have wronged you.

Although many will argue (articulately and successfully) that revenge magic has its place, it is a practice best left to the skilled and experienced magical workers. The idea remains constant, and is one of the few things agreed upon by most religions, that what you do comes back to you in varying degrees of severity. For many paths, it is a "threefold" factor: "Bread throw upon the waters of life comes back to you threefold" or "The Law of Three."

This means that whatever you put out into the Universe comes back to you and draws a similar experience to you. Therefore, if you enact a magic process that you know in your heart is going to bring harm to another, an override occurs that duplicates the magic and brings it back to you, some believe in triplicate. This stopgap measure keeps us in a mindset of sending out only positive magical work rather than what could be a harmful practice.

Working Energy Magic to control the life or actions of another person takes a tremendous amount of personal energy. The effect, if the Universe does not override your efforts and there is any at all, is normally very short-lived and comes at great personal costs (intentionally plural). It is always best to shape your Energy Magic work around free will choices and opportunities for the other person rather than direct control. Failure to do so can seriously undermine your efforts to achieve a positive result, which should always be your ultimate goal for the situation.

At the beginning of this particular section, we talked about the influence of free will, greatest good, and fate. A word we can add to those very powerful allies of the magical working person is "Karma." We identify those forces as allies because they really do help us to stay on the straight and narrow and provide a very effective corrective course when things threaten to go out of whack and head down a path that is not for our own greatest good.

Karma is a strong premise that embraced by nearly all organized and disorganized religions to some degree. We have a tremendous accountability for our own actions and to some degree, our thoughts, because as we have seen, thought is the beginning of the manifestation of form. Karma tells us that what we do affects not only others, but ourselves. When you get to be somewhere between middle age and old, you have lived enough years to see Karma come back around and balance out the scales many times.

There is a scene in the 1984 film *The Karate Kid* where Daniel Laruso, our protagonist, has repeatedly had the crap beaten out of him by a group of jocks who are part of the local karate dojo. Daniel exacts his own temporary revenge by turning on a water hose that has been pushed over the top of a bathroom stall in which his primary nemesis is preparing to smoke a joint. As Daniel runs past his new girlfriend with the angry and wet Cobra Kai teen hot on his heels, Daniel yells, "It's comin' around!"

Karma is like that. If you wait long enough, it will "come around" and we have rarely seen it fail. The Universe is a perfect, self-correcting process and whether we take action to assure that Justice spoons out or we wait patiently, rest assured that the scales will balance. The idea is that we do not want to be the ones who are getting wet in the bathroom stall, so be sure to stay on the good side of Karma because it bites with sharp teeth.

To be completely honest, in the three plus decades that we have been Energy Magic practitioners, we have approached the idea of Justice in many ways. We have actively sought Justice through magic and had it work well, but found that the guidance given to us many years about by a wise mentor held true: "Justice splatters." Our teacher was clear that when you invoke the idea of Justice, you had better be prepared because it *spills everywhere*. Unless you are beyond reproach and in total karmic balance (and really, who is?), be prepared when you invoke Justice because your own wrongs and hidden errors will be brought to light and called into accountability.

The responsible and safe approach if you feel you need to take magical action is to identify the issue as you see it and ask that it be handled in a way that results in the greatest good for all concerned. Ask for the protection of those who are innocent and that those who are guilty be shown their error and given the chance to make amends. This practice does not specify any particular person and gives The Universe a wide area in which to work. As with all magical work, once you have put this before The Goddess, step away knowing She will manage the situation most effectively and your input is no longer required on any level other than making your own amends should they present.

Do not contaminate your own magical process by bringing control and negativity into it. Leave the dirty work for The Universe and you will not have any regrets as the situation plays out. It may take time, but rest assured that the Karmic scale will balance and if you are lucky, you will be around to watch it happen.

## Working Without Permission

Many people will ask, "*Do you mind if I pray for you?*" This is a very gracious and respectful request. We cannot count, however, the number of prayer requests we receive through (usually mass mailed) emails or on Facebook that go something like this:

"*Dear Saints. Please pray for my brother who [fill in the blank here with 'lost his job,' 'is going through a divorce,' 'has diabetes,' 'is having surgery' etc]. He is a good person and does not deserve for this to happen.*"

We have to wonder whether this person has permission to harness a large number of people together in an effort to change someone's life in a significant way. As mentioned previously, when you orchestrate a group effort, it amplifies the effect is tremendously.

At first glance, we would assume that anyone would appreciate a giant influx of positive energy designed to make his or her life better. On the other hand, we do not know what the target of all of this energy wants, needs, or thinks. We know what *the person asking on their behalf* wants. As part of our upcoming chapter where we discuss how to live a magical life and bring all of this Energy Magic together into a cohesive, balanced life, we will talk about how selective we must be in deciding where we put our energy.

"Pray for all of the people who lost their homes in the tsunami." "Pray for all of the hungry people." "Pray for all of the homeless people." "Pray for our troops." "Pray for the President." Every day, we are inundated with requests to spend our prayer tokens on others, sometimes en masse. This is in addition to the time we spend praying for what we need for ourselves.

As with medical decisions, if a person is unconscious and unable to specify their wishes, it is reasonable for someone who knows them well to make choices on their behalf. If, however, the person is awake, aware, and conscious, then they should always give permission before such an effort takes place. After all, as with medical procedures, it is something that greatly affects *their own life*. No one should initiate this type of healing without the permission of the recipient.

When someone asks you to pray for someone else, it is appropriate to ask, "Do you have permission from this person to ask me to pray for them?" It is also very appropriate to pray for a person without their permission, but amend to the prayer to say, "I ask that the greatest good come forward for this person in their hour of need." This does not identify a specific outcome for the person other than what God determines their greatest good to be. This lends positive energy without contributing directive energy.

You should never take it upon yourself to decide what another person needs or wants. If someone asks you to work on their behalf, ask them specifically what outcome they want to see happen. If nothing else, this could take away generalities in their own minds and get them to focus on a specific outcome they desire.

A lack of clarity about where your energy is directed and why, as well as sending energy toward a target that may or may not want the end goal you are creating, is a good way to create conflict and obstacles in the successful accomplishment of your goal.

It is very helpful when the target of your prayers connects into your energy process and is responsible about its use. This creates a different sort of dynamic than the usual "funnel energy into the cause nonstop" approach.

Katrina once had a woman ask her to pray for her father-in-law, a Methodist minister, who was ill in the hospital. Katrina asked if she had permission for her to work for the sick man and the woman assured her that yes, he had given permission. Katrina lit a purple (purple supports energies of "the highest and the best") candle for him, sending healing energy into the candle. She took it out into her garage and placed it on a very high shelf to burn. At the time, she had small children and wanted the candle to burn without interruption for the full five days.

Two days later, she went into the garage and saw that the candle was out, but there was still wax in the glass container and the wick was uncovered and available as if it had been blown out. There were no drafts in the garage and the candle had been undisturbed.

She feared the worst and called her friend to check on her father-in-law. He had seen marked improvement and been discharged from the hospital that morning. He said to Josefa, "Tell your friend that I appreciate her prayers so very much, but I am better now and she can use that energy elsewhere." From a distance, several towns away, the man put out his own healing candle.

One would think that healing energy would be a given and would always be appropriate; therefore, asking permission to do it would be irrelevant. As a higher thinking person, however, there are other factors we must consider:

*What if this person is supposed to learn something important from their illness?*

*What if the illness is for the person's greatest good? (Such as a person who has been working far too hard and needs the rest)*

*What if the person does not, on some level, want to get better right now? (Such as a person who needs the attention the illness brings)*

*What if the illness is intended to bring attention to a different illness in the body that can be managed if detected right now. (Such as a cancer that is found on a detailed examination for a different set of symptoms)*

We never know why the Universe does things the way it does and therefore, it is always best to ask permission first and to add, "If it is for the greatest good" at the end of the magical prayer or work.

# Chapter 9 - Properties of Energy – In Summation

When you work without a specific direction for your energy to flow, the energy becomes diversified and scattered. The strongest energy follows a straight line toward one target and it is up to you, the person sending out the energy, to identify that target and clear the obstacles to get to it.

If you want to achieve the most positive results to your Energy Magic process:

*Identify a clear goal, using the ideas presented in this chapter.*

*Use some of the tools and actions described in the first section of this chapter to amplify your energy.*

*Use the ideas from the second part of this chapter to remove obstacles to your positive flow of energy.*

*Use the techniques specified in the next chapter to "bring it all together" into a spiritually based life and to create a ritual that supports what it is that you specifically want to accomplish.*

# Chapter 10 - Bringing It All Together

Given all that we have covered so far in this book about the nature of God, the neutrality and properties of energy, the definition and benefit of Bio-Universal energy, and the power of intention, the question then comes: "How do I actually *do* it?"

The beauty of Energy Magic is that there is no specific formula to follow. There is no guidance by fear of error or set of arcane rules. Think of Energy Magic as a concert that goes on in Nature and has played since the dawn of time. The music is beautiful and inviting. It never, ever stops. You pick up your instrument (your own bio-energy), slip into your seat, and begin to play along with the rest of the energies out there. What you contribute will be a lovely addition. You finish your part of the concert and then you slip away while the concert continues behind you.

There are many religions in the world that want people to believe that interacting with God, The Goddess, The Universe, Creator, The Divine, is a complicated process fraught with danger. Perhaps this works for them on some level. Many people love to feel they have completed a complex and treacherous journey to get to the "inner circle" where communion with The Almighty occurs. If that helps a person to feel more in touch with his or her Higher Self and more connected on a spiritual level, then we applaud their journey. Some churches insist that you must have a minister or a priest to mediate between you and God. Some Pagan paths feel there are you must be of a particular level of experience to have direct contact to God.

It is our impression over more than thirty years of Energy Magic practice and over forty years of dealing directly with God, that God is there for us in any capacity, at any time. We can do more to increase our own energy into a situation and blend it with Universal energy, but God is always there for us.

Since we started working directly with Energy Magic in 1996, we have had many well-intending ceremonial folks give us wild-eyed, hysterical warnings about handing this information over to "non-initiates." Phrases like "You're giving a baby a gun" and "It's like driving on the wrong side of the road" are flung around in response to our proposal that anyone can effectively work with Divine energy.

Upon further conversation, we ask them to explain to us exactly what they believe will happen if "ordinary" people know how to use Energy Magic. What is the "big bad" that will occur? So far, no one has given us a reasonable answer other than, "it will just be really bad." We have never once seen a result that was ultimately negative come from anyone working with Energy Magic. We have seen people from almost all spiritual paths improve their lives on an ongoing basis and develop and intimate and rewarding relationship with God. We have seen people mature into lovely, talented magical practitioners who trust in "the process" and feel tremendous peace knowing that they are empowered to create the life and future they want most.

Energy Magic is a beautiful and sacred practice that awakens the Higher Self in its practitioners and brings the holy and blessed experiences into our lives more frequently and in a stronger capacity. If you apply yourself to the process, you will truly live the ordinary life in an extraordinary way.

Think back on some of the premises we discussed and imagine how you can use the ideas of what speeds up bio-energy and what slows it down. The Universal energy that comes from The Goddess is eternal and steady. It does not wax and wane. It is always there. Our ability to feel it and benefit from it is often limited by the distance we have put between The Divine and ourselves. Many times, we stop listening to God because we do not like what God is saying. In short, we do not get our way, things do not progress as we feel they should, so we blame God and walk away.

Since the energy of God is a constant, the variable is our own bio-energy. As you have read, many factors may affect its flow and probably will in the course of human life. We are likely to get sick. We will sometimes have clutter and chaos around us. We will be tired on occasion. It is a given.

Ideally, we surround ourselves with beautiful, sacred items in our home to keep us in a spiritual mindset. We take care of our bodies because of the vital connection between the spirit, the mind, and the body. If the body becomes compromised, the spirit and mind will follow almost immediately. By honoring our physical bodies, we keep ourselves healthier, which allows us to have greater energy to invest on all levels.

Keep incense, fragrant oils, potpourri, candles, and other sacred scents in your environment and learn how the different aromas influence you. Discover which ones calm you and which ones increase your energy. Which ones make you feel most alive, most spiritual, most grounded, and most connected?

What visual cues keep you in a spiritual mindset? For us, representations of dragons with their magical might accomplishes this, so there are dragon figures scattered throughout our home. We enjoy images of Kwan Yin, the Goddess who insists that She will not enter Heaven until all her children are safely inside, also gives her comfort. Seeing pentacles, the representation of the earthly elements (Earth, Air, Fire, and Water) created by God from which all things are formed and forced, crowned by Sprit and joined together by the circle of life causes us to feel magical and balanced. As you begin to identify your magical visual cues, make sure you surround yourself with them in the areas you most frequent.

# Chapter 11 - Take Back Your Power Eggs

Be ruthless about eliminating drama in your life. Identify the people in your life who lift you up and make you smile and those who drain away your energy. Distance yourself from those energy black holes and vampire we discussed in the previous chapters.

Some wise guidance to consider is that the true measure of a person is how you feel when you are walking away from them. Do you feel energized, happy, and supported or do you feel drained, exhausted, or used? Do not think twice about drastically reducing contact with those who do not help you to feel amazing.

In Katrina's life coach sessions, she has a favorite saying. "Re-establish the dancing distance." You do not have to make a major production of "breaking up" with people who are a drain to your energy. You simply stop being available for their dumping. If you must see them, wait until you have an energy surplus and can handle the drain. Do not take the calls. Do not buy into the drama. Do not be manipulated through guilt. You owe it to yourself and those who love you to be the best "you" you can be and that means valiantly protecting where your energy goes.

At first, they may bemoan your lack of availability and even up their drama to try and draw you in. Be assured that when they do not get the reaction they seek, which usually involves the complete cessation of your world so that you can wrap around their world, they will move on to others who will accommodate their need for attention. Meanwhile, it is unlikely you will lose the relationship. People like that hate to burn bridges, despite threats. You will, however, maintain the integrity of knowing you are being careful about where you energy goes.

Some Native American tribes call this, *"Taking back your power eggs."* Consider the fact that our energy is finite. We do not have an unlimited flow and after a period in energy deficit, our systems on all three levels, Spirit, Mind, and Body, will start to break down. If we give away our energy carelessly to those who do not deserve it and sometimes, to those who do, we will eventually end up compromised on those three levels. That is why it is essential that we preserve our energy, sending it only to targets where we know it will be effective.

It is like having a table that supported by three legs. If you cut one of the legs short by a few inches, the rest of the legs will suffer and the stability of the table becomes compromised. All three must be in balance for the table to be stable. If you attempt to gain stability by cutting down the other three legs, the table may be in balance and stable, but it will get shorter and shorter and will likely never again sit as level or as stable as it did originally. If, however, you build up the short leg instead of cutting down the other legs, you have a better chance at achieving a good balance.

How many times have you had the exact same argument with a friend repeatedly and never had it go anywhere that is productive? How often do people call to vent to you about how horrible their life is, yet they refuse to do anything about it? How many times do you hear someone bemoaning how awful their life is and you quickly realize that they do not want solutions, they want to be comforted for being a victim? These are all examples of wasted energy.

How many times do you say "yes" you will do something for someone else, when you really want to say no? How much of your ego gets tied up in being indispensible to others? How often do you feel used or place expectations on others without their knowledge, only to feel disadvantaged and resentful when they fail to live up to the standards you set for them in your mind?

All these situations are unnecessary energy drains Distancing yourself from people who sap your energy in no way means you do not love them. It means you love YOU enough to not set up an unbalanced relationship that leaves you feeling depleted.

When you find yourself starting to sigh a lot in conversations or feel as if you wish you were somewhere else, stop and excuse yourself. You do not have to be rude or dismissive. Simply say, "You know, I just realized something I need to do and I am going to have to cut this short." If they protest or even beg for your attention, kindly tell them that you need some time and then take that time. If they do not give it to you, then it is clear they are not responsive to your needs and that too is a problem.

You are the only one who can stop the extraneous energy flow that goes to these black holes. Barring death, the person on the receiving end will, work hard to preserve the status quo because it is of benefit to them. You are the one who has to change the dynamic and "take back your power eggs." Reel in the energy that is scattered in nonproductive directions.

Careful and judicious management of your energy flow is a very, very big part of Energy Magic. So often, we are casual about where our energy goes, but the very fact that you are reading these words means that it is time for this message to come to you. It is time to plug up the leaks.

# Chapter 12 - The River Meditation

What follows is a brilliant meditation developed Eric for visualizing your energy flow and plugging up the leaks.

Settle yourself into a comfortable position where your body is well supported and you do not have to consciously think about holding yourself upright. Wiggle your body around a bit to settle into your position.

Take several deep breaths, in the nose and out the mouth. Feel the air circulate through your body, bringing with it the essentials it needs to be healthy and nourished. Continue to breathe rhythmically and deeply, saturating yourself with healthy oxygen and breath. Rest your hands so that they are in the "receive" position with palm open and up or near up.

As you take each breath, feel yourself become more and more relaxed. Your larger limbs become heavier and heavier with each exhalation. Your body parts relax: your legs, your pelvis, your back, your abdomen and chest, your shoulders, your neck, and your face. Pull in a breath for each of these body parts and feel them become heavy as you exhale.

Once your body is fully relaxed, still your mind. Picture the thoughts as tangible objects, moving around in your head. See their motion slow and then see them fall softly to the floor around you.

*Imagine that you stand on the riverbank next to a river. Your river may be raging or it could be softly moving. The water level may be high or low. Go with the very first imagery you receive. That is your authentic image.*

*Toward the head of the river, there is a dam. The dam is as tall as you envision it to be. There are floodgates in the dam that operated by wheels that are turned. There is tremendous water pressure behind the dam that you access by turning the wheels and letting more water through the floodgates.*

*This river is your own personal energy. If you saw the river as low and slow, then your personal energy needs work. If you saw it as strong and forceful, you may need to slow it down a bit. The energy behind the dam is Universal energy from God/The Goddess/The Universe.*

*Turn your attention to the mouth of the river below. How much water has actually made it to the bottom? What is the condition of the water? Is it murky and ugly? Is it pure and clean? Is it green? Blue? Brown? Clear?*

*In between the dam and the mouth of your river, there are a number of tributaries. Small creeks branch off your main river and divert some of the water to other places. These tributaries have names identified by signs stuck in the bank beside them. Everyone will have his or her own signs. Some will have the names of people. Some will have "work," or "health concerns," or "finances." You will have a tributary for every place that drains away your energy. The water you have at the mouth of the river represents what you have in reserve at the end.*

*You have complete control over your river. There is work that needs to be done. You can do it yourself or you can envision that you bring workers in to do it for you. It does not matter how it gets done, but during your meditation, it should be completed.*

*The first course of action is to block off the tributaries you no longer wish to feed. If you do not want your energy to go to that place any longer, then patch up the "hole" that lets the water/energy through. Slowly and carefully, mend every outlet that you do not want to use any longer. Widen outlets where you want to devote more energy. Take your time with this process.*

*Once you are satisfied that all of your energy/water is going where you want it to go, return to the dam and open the floodgates to let a little or a lot of Universal energy flow into your river. This will help to fortify you and your energy flow.*

*See the water that comes from the floodgates as clear, pure, and strong. It is eager to get through the openings in the dam and practically shoves its way into your river, eager to revitalize you and get your river moving at a healthy pace. It cleanses away any old, stagnant water that is there.*

*Spend some time with your river for a few minutes. Check out specifics that are only for you in your vision. Lie beside the river for a while and listen to it flow, confident that all of that water and energy is going to the proper places. See that you now have a nice surplus of water all the way down to the end of the river, as far as you can see.*

Once you have completed your river time, let the darkness behind your closed eyes envelope you once again. Feel the awareness begin to return to your body parts from your toes, all the way up your limbs and torso, to your head.

Gently open your eyes, and spend a few moments considering the images you just saw and what they mean to you. You can return to the river meditation as often as you want. Sometimes, all is well and you just want to rest by your river. Other times, great work is needed. You will know what to do and when to do it.

# Chapter 13 - Pray and/or Meditate

Take time to be alone with God every single day without fail. Treat that time as an essential part of your day that is as important as personal hygiene, eating, exercise, and breathing. This does not have to be an elaborate process. Simply take a few minutes to relax, take a few deep breaths, and allow yourself to connect in with Spirit. Clear your mind of all drama, all fear, all problem-solving, and let only peace and joy come in. Recognize that in that handful of minute, there is nothing you can do and nothing you *must* do to change anything. Realize that God sees you as perfect the way you are. For those moments, give yourself permission simply to *be* without attaching any expectations or assumptions onto the process. Just let time pass around you and sit with your inner peace for a while.

This is different from the times when you go into Higher Self to affect a change. You are not asking for anything at this time. You are simply sitting with Universal Energy and sharing time. You know those friends who only come around when they want something from you? Do not establish that type of relationship with God. Make certain to share time without expectations on a regular basis. As you relax, slip deeper inside yourself or go the other direction and rise above your body reaching upward with your own Spirit. Find the direction that feels right to you. See how quiet you can make your mind. Sit in the quietness for a while.

There are many wonderful meditative guides available on CD and MP3 formats. Some have both instructional information and guided meditations, similar to the River Meditation in the previous section. These will help you if you are a novice and need practice. Meditation is an art that takes time to learn.

Through daily practice, you will begin to notice levels to your meditative process related to the types of brain waves going on in your head. Beta waves are the ones in which we normally function. This is our awake, aware, fully conscious, plugged-into-outside-stimuli waves.

As we move deeper into meditation, we experience Alpha waves, which put us into a dreamy, passive, and receptive state. After Alpha, we move into Theta waves, which are a very deep relaxation state in which we are extremely creative. Our thoughts begin to move spontaneously through different worlds and show you pictures, much like watching a movie. With practice, you can slow down and speed up the images you see. Sometimes, they are relevant and sometimes, they seem like entertainment. Expert meditators are able to get to the coveted Delta waves, which are the deepest form of meditation in which we almost seem to be unconscious. Our intuition and insight are very high in this phase and this is the strongest connection between people and God. Hypnosis is most effective when the subject is in a Theta and Delta wave state.

If you are a beginner, it is sufficient to sit quietly and still your mind. Do not be surprised if your shoulders or other body parts twitch as relaxation settles into them. For most people, it is rare that they seek out active relaxation. This is different from the passive relaxation that is the onset of sleep. In this case, you are still mentally active on varying levels. Your body is becoming very relaxed and still. Your mind will be still of Beta-wave thoughts. Once you are able to let go of your attachment to the outside world, the imagery of Theta and Delta waves is free to begin.

When you pray at this time, make it a process of thanks and communion. Send out your gratitude for the blessings in your life and cultivate your extreme understanding that all is right in the process and that you are exactly where you are meant to be.

Protect your quiet time every day. This can be 15 minutes or even longer. Every day, you will find your connection to The Divine deepening during your meditative moments.

# Chapter 14 - Ritual for Results

As we mentioned before, all religions use ritual to connect to God. Some recite the liturgy, some sing the Doxology, some bow and pray, some eat and drink specific items or observe a ritual fasting time. Ritual is the core of connectivity to The Universe/The Divine.

One of the messages ritual conveys to us, both through our Higher Self and our Conscious Self, is that this is an intentional, concerted act to take seriously. From the beginning of ritual until the end, we identify a time in our day that is a specific activity designed to connect to your most sacred self and to God.

Ritual does not have to be a fully formalized occasion. It can be a ritual bath with fragrant oils or herbs, candles lit and quiet music playing as you cleanse yourself of negative energy and impurities. Our book *The Art of Ritual Crafting* provides detailed instructions for creating a meaningful ritual, but the key points to include are:

*A specific beginning point*

*A directed goal of the ritual*

*A period of connecting into Deity*

*A period of energy building and output if it is appropriate to the goal*

*A period of grounding*

*A specific ending point*

What you do to achieve those six points is completely up to you. It is important to be gracious to Deity and any other energies you invite into your ritual area. Thank them for being there and giving you their support. There should never be a need for an Energy Magic practitioner to bring negative or harmful influences into their ritual space. People who are use magic as a means to boost their ego and control others will sometimes do this, but it has no place in what we do. Our emphasis is on the self and taking action to make our own lives better.

Speaking of being gracious and thankful, it is perfectly fine to create a ritual with the purpose of saying thank you for all you have received. It is interesting that the "Law of Three" works for the good as well as the negative. If you put gratitude, love, and joy out there into the world, that is also what comes back to you in varying degrees.

Some people enjoy erecting a circle around them as a magical working area. This is perfectly fine if that is what makes you feel comfortable. The usual purpose for working within a circle is to "cut away" a sacred space from the mundane world, to contain the energy you build up until you release it, and to provide a degree of protection either from factors outside of the circle or from what you may bring into the circle.

The last issue should not be a problem if you followed the guidelines previous addressed. You should always work magic in a secure, comfortable place where you feel at ease and are not likely to encounter interruptions. You should not work a type of magic that will bring unsavory energy into your circle from which you need protection.

If the type of energy you are working has an activity, such as a "Cone of Power" to raise energy before sending it out into the world, a designated circle area can be useful. If it helps you to envision that you separate your magical working area from the outside world, a circle can be helpful for that as well. For ourselves, sometimes we use a circle and other times, we do not.

To cast a circle, simply use your hand, a wand of some kind, or a knife or sword of any kind, and draw an area around you that is roughly circular and big enough to surround the work area you plan to use. You can literally draw a circle with chalk on the floor or trace one in the air symbolically.

During the time your circle is in place, you do not step over it or leave the circle without first drawing a door to exit and going through the motion of closing it behind you and reopening it when you return. This is to maintain the mental integrity of an actual circle of energy existing around you. The same applies if others want to enter or exit the circle. All should remain within the confines of the circle. Animals and children are irrelevant to circle integrity, so do not worry if they cross the circle boundaries.

When your ritual is complete, do not forget to take down your circle, by imagining that you draw it back up into your hand, wand, sword, knife, etc, in the opposite direction from which you laid it down. If you have a permanent working circle made of rocks, tape on the floor or other items, make a door in the circle for leaving and returning.

# Chapter 15 - Acts of Focus

During your ritual, the act of focusing your attention on the task at hand is critical to a successful output of energy. Scattered attention equals scattered energy. In the section on the Properties of Energy, we discussed several things that speed up the flow of energy. Use them to increase your focus and energy levels while working in your magical ritual space.

## A Homemade Rosary: Knot Magic

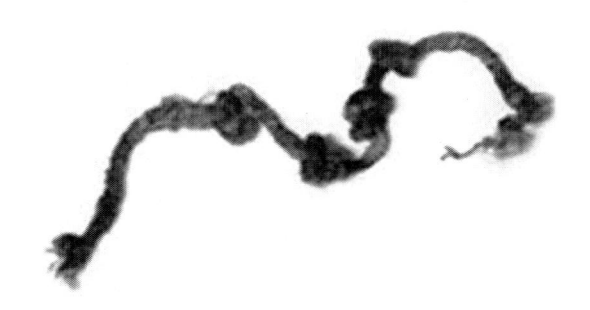

"Knot Magic." is a very effective form of focused magic similar to praying the rosary, except that you are instilling your own intent into each "bead," which is actually a knot.

Get a length of narrow cord that is strong enough that it does not break as you pull on it. It can be of any substance that feels nice in your hands and moves smoothly as you tie it off.

In front of you, put a representation of what you want to achieve. It can be a unit of currency if you are working for money, a photo if you are helping a friend (with permission!), a symbol of love if you want to draw in love, etc. Visual cues help to keep us focused.

With your goal firmly in mind, measure out a length of the cord that is as long as the distance from your elbow to the tip of your middle finger. This will further personalize your work.

Holding the cord in your hands and focusing on your visual cue, tie off a knot each time you say a line of the following:

*By knot of one, the work's begun (tie the first knot)*

*By knot of two, it cometh true (tie the second knot)*

*By knot of three, it comes to me (continue with each knot)*

*By knot of four, unlock the door*

*By knot of five, it comes alive*

*By knot of six, the work is fixed*

*By knot of seven, my will to heaven*

*By knot of eight, it's looking great*

*By knot of nine, this work is mine*

*By knot of ten, the work will end.*

When you tie your tenth knot, use it to tie one end of the cord to the other to bring it into a circle. In the course of this work, you begin the work, identify your goal, send it to The Universe, claim the goal as a completed act, then end the work.

The energy that is tied into this cord will be released when the final (10$^{th}$) knot is untied or when you burn the cord. This work can contain the energy of certain events, like a Full Moon, an eclipse, a storm, or other high-energy moments. You can then release the energy later when it is needed.

## Focus Bags

Focus bags can be made of any material and hold symbols and tokens that are sympathetic to your goal. The bag itself is usually quite small, maybe the size of a golf ball or slightly larger. Into the bag, you put herbs that compliment your goal, tokens such as charms, or other tiny items, stones that work toward the goal you want to accomplish, plus anything else that supports what you want to manifest.

You then bless the bag toward your goal by praying with it in your hands and sending your energy for the goal into the bag. Keep the bag on your altar or other sacred space, in your pocket, or even in your clothes close to your body. Some people wear their focus bags around their neck on a cord or tie them to a staff or other magical item. Another name for a focus bag is a "mojo bag."

# Working Candles

Because of its porous nature, wax is a wonderful material for storing energy. Candles have long been used for sacred work of all kinds from complex magical work to simply "lighting a candle" for someone.

The candle you choose can be as elaborate or as plain as you like. The fanciness of the candle in no way affects the performance. It is all about the energy you put into it. You do not have to use a new candle for magical work. Just put the candle under running water (from the tap is fine) and ask that the water cleanse away any negativity and impurities and leave the candle as a clean and empty vessel.

Choose a candle that is of the appropriate supporting color to your goal. Check the list in the appendix for some guidelines. Remember that the size of the candle will usually be the determining factor in how long it burns. If you want something to happen quickly, use a birthday candle or tea light. If you want to work on this project over time, use a thicker, taller candle. There is no hard and fast rule on the benefit of tapers, votives, column candles, beeswax, soy candles, or paraffin.

Anoint your magical working candle with oil that is sympathetic to your work. Again, see the list in the appendix for herbs or premade oil that are in line with your goal. To anoint a candle, use your index finger dipped in oil to circle the center of the candle as if it wore a belt of oil. Once a heavily oiled "belt" is around the candle, hold the candle in both of your hands with your thumbs and index fingers toward the center of the candle. Using a twisting motion, pull to the left with your left hand and to the right with your right hand, distributing the oil smoothly over the surface of the candle. If the candle is too large to "dress" in this fashion, just use your hands to spread oil from the center out to each end. This effectively moves the energy of the oil throughout the candles.

You may carve or write on the candle as you please to personalize it, although it is not necessary.

Once the candle is dressed and ready, hold it in your hands and still your mind. Create a strong image of your goal and see it as already complete. Imagine exactly how you will feel and react once the goal is accomplished. Be as detailed as possible when you create this thoughtform. Once you have this image firmly in your mind, use your mind to *push* the image into the soft wax of the candle.

When you have effectively instilled the image of your goal into the candle, you are free to light it and release the energy. You may do so all at once, burning the candle down completely in one sitting as long as it is in a safe, fire-free location. You may burn the candle for a while and let the energy go out, then blow out the candle and burn it more on another day.

There are many traditions around candle use, most of which we have found to be without consequence. People will warn others to never to use candles that have been used for a different purpose. We have never found this to be a problem. We simply clean them out with the water trick and reuse them.

We have been told that candles must always be blown out or snuffed or pinched out. Everyone has a different explanation for why their own preferred method is superior. We just put the thing out and we have never noticed a consequence for the method we used.

People will warn others that they should always use new candles and never buy candles in thrift stores. A good 90% of the candles we use for Energy Magic come from thrift stores, used or new. We have never had a negative result and again, just use the water trick and purge the candle of existing energy, then fill it up with our own intent.

People enjoy their superstitions, but we are thrifty practitioners and money counts to us. We do not engage our magical process from a position of fear and the flashlight under the chin. Everyone creates their own magical experience and as that develops over time, they get to determine whether their magical journey will be fraught with boogiemen and danger or simple and serene. We are more of KISS people (Keep It Simple, Sweetie). In all our years as practitioners, we have never once suffered for this approach. Katrina's mother used to call such fearfulness, "Seeing demons behind clothesbaskets."

From a practical standpoint, please follow the following safety tips:

> *Be sure your candle flame is away from any potential inferno creating material.*
>
> *Do not use a wooden candleholder unless it has a brass inset that will keep it from catching fire.*
>
> *Be careful with glass containers for candles as some of them will crack under heat.*
>
> *One of the safest ways to burn a taper is to stick it into a container of sand.*
>
> *Votive candles must be burned in a votive holder as they tend to not hold shape and puddle as they burn.*
>
> *Column candles have layers in their construction with a harder outer layer that usually does not burn.*
>
> *Candles burned near a breeze, fan, or other source of moving air will burn much faster and unevenly. Make sure your burning candle is protected from moving air.*
>
> *Never leave candles burning unattended unless they are glass jar candles, which are generally safe.*

Five-day candles, available in the Hispanic food section of many grocery stores and dollar stores, are wonderful for use in Energy Magic work. They come in a variety of colors and many have images on them that make great focus cues. White is a universal color that can be used for any purpose, so if you find one you like and the color is white, it will work beautifully. These candles burn for around five days and are safe to leave burning unattended provided you have them away from anything flammable. We dress the top of the candle with oil using a fingertip.

## Wills & Petitions

When most people think of a will, they think of a "Last Will and Testament." In this case, we are talking about a written statement of your own will that you wish to have enacted. As we previously covered, the written word is a powerful tool and putting something into writing gives it a certain substance over it simply flying around inside your head. We associate writing with "proof" and "contracts," which helps us to lend a sense of legitimacy to the written word. It creates a feeling of permanence and credibility, which is why we have phrases such as "There it is! Right there in black and white!"

As we all well know, just because something appears in print does not make it so. Our own mental framework creates the legitimacy and credibility we assign to written works. By this token, our mental processes respond well to ideas that put down on paper. We will react faster to a list that is staring us down than we do to the same tasks we know we have to perform that are mental notes rather than physical ones.

To create a magical will or petition, we recommend finding a quiet place where you will not be disturbed. Think carefully about what you want to manifest as your goal and then put it in writing. You can be as specific as you want to be, but the flow of your Energy Magic will be stronger if you give The Universe room to operate.

If you want reliable, attractive transportation for a price you can easily afford, that is a goal with a lot of room for variables to come into play. If you want a 1969 dark blue Ford Mustang in prime condition for $1000, that is going to take a little longer and require more energy. Meanwhile, the 1971 red mustang for $900 slips right past you.

For this reason, it is highly advisable that you focus on the feeling you want to have when you accomplish your goal rather than the absolute specifics. Some time ago, Katrina's son did Energy Magic work to bring the perfect woman into his life. He wrote a list (a will) of all of the attributes he wanted in this perfect woman – things like "a good sense of humor," "a career she loves," "an interest in movies," etc. He lit a red candle (for passion), put his list under the candle, and waited. Over the course of the next few weeks, Katrina received a series of phone calls from her son. "Mom, she's perfect, but I forgot to put 'not married' on the list." "Mom, she's perfect, but I forgot to put 'not a lesbian' on the list." "Mom, she's perfect, but I forgot to put 'Not crazy' on the list."

Had he focused on a particular set of feelings he wanted to have in the relationship (security, love, availability, passion, mutuality, pride, shared joyfulness), the door would have opened for someone to fill that role without needing to be so specific.

Once you have identified exactly what you want to accomplish with your Energy Magic, put it to paper. Some people like to offer up a sacrifice for their reward. This no longer takes the form of animal, human, or blood sacrifice as it once did for nearly all religions. Now it is an offering in return to the Universe in return. You might offer to meditation every day for 30 minutes for a week, work at a homeless shelter, or create a flower garden space in honor of your goal. Your offering can be as selfless or complex as you choose. The Universe does not require an offering or sacrifice from you, but in our human minds, we see it as balancing the scales. It is completely to your preference. The energy of that sacrifice then goes to fuel the "bio" energy that you contribute to the Energy Magic duet.

When you have finished writing your will, check it over to make sure it says exactly what you want to say. Include a codicil that says something to the effect of, "I ask for the equal of this or better and I ask as it harms none and is in conjunction with the greatest good."

Sign your will and once you have done so, you are free to use it as you choose. Most people prefer to burn it. You can roll it into a tube and seal it with candle wax, fold it into an origami figure or just a simple square, tie it with a string, or whatever you like. It is fine to bless the will with oils that are sympathetic to your goal, much as you did the candle or just touching your oiled fingertip to the paper. If you fold the will, you can include powdered incenses or herbs inside the folds to boost the energy.

In a fire safe area, light the will using the flame of a candle, match, or lighter. Drop the will into the fire safe burning area and watch it burn. The way the will burns tells you a lot about how the work will go. If it burns quickly and hungrily, your will is hard at work and will likely enact quickly. If it burns slowly and thoughtfully, it may take longer, but will go well. If parts of the will do not burn or are difficult to catch fire, your will may need to be refined. If your will does not burn well at all, take a breath and wait until another day. Let the world turn a time or two and then try again.

## Poppets

Poppets are another type of focus tool that help you direct your energy. There is a pattern in the appendix of this book that you can trace onto typing paper to make your own poppet.

The first idea most people get when the see a poppet is that of a voodoo doll used to harm others. Poppets are merely a focus tool to direct your energy to a particular person. Since we already know the ethics involved with energy movement and the Law of Three, you know that any use of a poppet or other magical tool for harm to others will generate negative results.

In this case, we can use a poppet for good. Trace the pattern onto paper. You will need to "cut two," so make sure the fabric you use is twice the size of the poppet pattern then fold the fabric in half. Pin the poppet pattern onto the folded fabric so that it holds the paper and both layers of fabric in place. Cut around the fabric, following the outer outline of the poppet.

Once you have the figure cut out, unpin the pattern and fabric pieces, leaving the fabric pieces lined up. Using a needle with knotted thread, carefully stitch around the edges of the poppet with a simple, straight stitch. You will need to lose a space of maybe two inches between where you started the stitches and where you end them. Use this unsewn space to turn the poppet inside out.

Once you have done this, stuff the poppet with old stockings or panty hose, cotton, polyester filling, or whatever you choose. You can also sew herbs into the poppet that are sympathetic to your goal. After the poppet is full, use the needle and thread to close off the opening you used for turning and stuffing.

Now your poppet is almost complete. You can write the name of the person onto the poppet or put a photo of the person's face on its head. If you have samples of the person's hair, you can tape or sew that to the poppet or put them inside of it to personalize it further. You want to tie the Energy Magic you will enact as closely to the person as possible.

What you do next with the poppet depends on your goal. The most common use for a poppet in modern times is for healing. If a person had a painful back condition, for instance, you could turn the poppet over and begin rubbing its back gently and sending it soothing, healing energy. You can do the same for a headache, stomach condition, etc.

If you want to wish prosperity for someone, you can use your printer to print out copies of hundred dollar bills then rain them down over the poppet. If you wanted the person to find love, put them next to a picture that represents romance to you. Each day, move the poppet closer to the picture to symbolize drawing that energy to them. As always, never work Energy Magic for someone without his or her permission.

# Chapter 16 - Using Your Body Centers

In a previous chapter, we briefly discussed your body's power centers, the chakras. They are the generators of bio energy and the meridians are the pathways that carry it through your body. The lymphatic system is the filter that cleanses out negativity and blocked energy.

How can you interact with this incredible system to create a better energy flow? One way is to make sure your lymph nodes are stimulated and active. They are just above the creases of your legs, under the breasts and armpits and under and behind the jaw line.

If you gently massage these areas, you may feel some tenderness. This tells you that there is an energy blockage going on at that point. Gently massage the area until the tenderness is gone.

Body Brushing is a technique in which a dry brush, preferably with natural bristles, is rubbed over the skin toward the lymphatic points. This encourages energy toward those points and pushes it out. Practicing body brushing 3-4 times a week is a good way to keep the lymphatic system awake and active. It also makes your skin feel wonderful when you step into a shower immediately afterward.

Working with the chakras themselves can be a very rewarding experience. They tend to tell us where we are having difficulties physically and spiritually. A cardiac problem, for instance, can indicate an issue with the heart chakra.

Each of the chakra points governs a part of our being. The chakras are also each associated with a color:

The first chakra at your tailbone is red and is associated with your home, feelings of trust, your sexuality, and your feelings of belonging, of safety, and your sense of survival.

Your second chakra at your navel is orange and governs your relationships, your inter-dependencies, your boundaries, your ability to release, and your conflicts, inner and outer.

Your third chakra is at your solar plexus and it is yellow. It relates to your addictions, your self-esteem, your social identify, your responsibilities, and your feelings of inadequacy, as well as your desire for revenge.

Your fourth chakra is green and is at your heart level. It influences your passions, your capacity for compassion, your ability to nurture, your creative expression, and your emotional expression.

Your fifth chakra is at your throat and is blue. It is responsible for your communication – both listening and speaking skills, your ability to effectively comprehend, and your sense of timing.

Your sixth chakra is indigo and is at your third eye. It governs your sense of perception, your clarity, your intellect, your moral code, your level of repression, and your fears.

Your seventh chakra is at the top of your head and is violet. It gives you your life's purpose, your spiritual connection, your personal influence, and your connection to Universal Flow.

If you flood the chakra area with the color that is specific to it, either literally (such as filters over a flashlight) or visually (in meditation), it helps restore health to that area. You can also focus on the chakra area that is guardian over the territory you wish to address with your Energy Magic work. If you want to work on weight loss, use yellow colors and pull your energy from the third chakra area. If you want to find a new home, use red colors and pull from your root/base chakra. If you want to heal a relationship or overcome conflict, use orange colors and pull from the second chakra, etc.

# Chapter 17 - Call a Goddess/Saint!

Each of the saints is assigned an attribute that makes them particularly helpful. St. Anthony helps you find lost items. The following chant is very effective: *St. Anthony, St. Anthony, please look around! Something is lost and now must be found!*

St. Jude is the patron saint of lost causes and is a beautiful energy to work with when situations are most dire.

God and Goddesses throughout different cultures have been imbued with various attributes that grant them affinities for circumstances. Hesta is the Goddess of Hearth and Home and is a wonderful deity to approach when your home is in turmoil. Mercury is the God of communications and messages and is a fine source of support when you need to effectively communicate with others.

Research into the Patron Saints and the various faces humankind has assigned to God over the centuries can provide a comfortable place to be when our needs are specific to one area of their expertise.

Literally thousands of years have been invested into the energy of Saints, Gods, Goddesses, Angels, and other extensions of the power of God. The paths are well worn, friendly, and comforting. Remember that you are still engaging a part of God.

# Chapter 18 - Connect to God Through the Elements

In the first few words of this book, we mentioned a list of what we considered to be very common, but very sacred experiences. Many of them involve the natural elements of our planet, Earth: earth, air, fire, and water.

God is present in all of Nature, which is what allows it to sing with life. We often feel closest to God in natural environments such as the beach or the woods. We can use the elements to connect more closely to God. Below are listed some sample exercises you can use if you would like to get in closer touch with the elements and their individual energies.

## Earth

Earth is associated with the North and with healing, prosperity, and grounding. This interaction with earth should be done outside in comfortable weather when the moon is full. You will need:

*1 jar/vase of pure oil (olive, safflower, sunflower)*

*Powdered or loose incense that smells earthy*

*An incense burner appropriate for burning powdered incense*

*A self-igniting charcoal disk*

*4 large stones arranged in a circle to represent the directions.*

*Appropriate color quarter candles (shielded), to place at each stone (not on the stone)*

*Wooden matches*

*A bowl or saucer*

*A wand or ritual knife.*

Light the candles and draw a circle around the stones with your knife or wand. Place the incense burner in the North of your working area and light the self-igniting charcoal disk. Starting at the East, pour a small quantity of oil on the stone. Raise your arms to the sky and welcome the energy of air to the circle. Continue around the circle, calling element into the circle with fire in the South, water in the West, and ending with earth in the North. Do not invoke the energies to the earth yet. Kneel or sit comfortably in the North quarter, making sure your body is in contact with the earth. Place some of the powdered incense on the charcoal. While sitting, run your hands through the grass and earth around you. Feel the texture of the earth. Feel how cool or warm the earth feels. Rub the earth between your hands. Bring the earth to your nose and inhale its scent. Put a touch of the earth on your tongue and taste it.

Once you have spent several minutes communing with the earth, stand, and call the element of earth to the circle. What do you feel when you invite it is? Lie flat on your stomach; head pointed to the North, left arm to the West, and right arm to the East with your feet to the South. Feel the connection to the earth and let the energies of the earth flow up through your body. As you lay there, tell the Mother Earth what you need.

Whisper your request to the earth. Feel the energy move through your body and know that your needs will be met in abundance. Thank the Mother Earth for listening and caring for you. Thank Her for giving you a place to live, food to eat, Her healing powers and for providing a place to ground energies. Give your love and appreciation back to Her. Rise to a sitting position. Pour some of the remaining oil into the bowl or saucer. Add a handful of dirt to the oil and mix it with your fingers until it forms a thin paste. Using the dirt/oil mixture, bless your hands, feet, heart, and head. Take a few more minutes to commune with earth if you desire.

When you have finished, stand and thank the earth for its presence and energy. Put out the North candle. Pinch out the candles in reverse order, West, South and East. Depart the circle taking the candles with you. Wait fifteen minutes, then write down your impressions

## Air

Air is associated with the East and with intellect, new beginnings, and all types of enterprise. This exercise should be done outside in fair weather when the moon is full. You should wear flowing robes or garments. You will need:

*2 Hand fans*

*2 candles (1 to represent God, 1 You – Bio & Universal)*

*4 incense burners suitable for powdered incense to be burned on charcoal disks*

*A powdered incense that makes you feel aligned with the element of air*

*4 self-igniting charcoal disks*

*Music (light and airy, your choice)*

Start the music you have chosen. Draw the circle area around you. Place an incense burner in each of the 4 quarters and light charcoals in each one. Allow a few moments for them to heat well. Pause for a few minutes to meditate on the element of Air; what it means to you, and what it feels like to you. Invite God and Goddess to bear witness to and assist you with your rite. Light the candles as you call them. Walk the circle and ensure all charcoals are lit.

Beginning in the South, invite fire to be in your sacred circle as you put approximately a teaspoon of incense on the charcoal. At the West, invite water and at the North, invite earth. When you arrive in the East, invite air to be with you. What do you feel?

Use the fans to move the smoke of the incense. Begin to dance with the fans, allowing them to sweep incense-filled air all around you. Blend the rhythm of the dance with the incense fumes (there should be plenty) and the music you have chosen. Imagine that you become one with the incense and the air and the music. When dancing becomes labored, move to the circle center and drop to the ground. Allow yourself to blend with the incense, music and any breeze there might be. Clear your mind and allow yourself to meditate and drift and vision.

When you have finished, rise. Thank the elements for their energies, presence, and protection. Thank God for sharing this time with you through the air and extinguish the God candle. Close your eyes and draw in your own energy expended in the circle and put out the candle that represents you. Open the circle. Wait fifteen minutes then write about your feelings.

## Fire

Fire is affiliated with the South and with creativity, passion, and motivation. This exercise should be done outside during the New Moon. You should wear red. You will need:

*Milk & Honey, mixed together*

*Area for burning outside, such as stones for fire ring or top to BBQ grill, inverted, with grill rack inserted*

*Four largish stones to mark the four directions*

*Appropriate color quarter candles (shielded), to place on each stone*

*Lighter fluid*

*Wood, small and large pieces, dry (Dabble minimally with lighter fluid before ritual)*

*A small fire starter log*

*Wooden matches*

*A powdered or loose incense that makes you feel aligned with the element of fire*

*Salt Peter*

*Lightweight writing paper and a pen*

*Your knife or wand*

Place the directional stones in a nice size circle around you. Using your knife or wand, draw a circle in the earth the size of your fire area or BBQ lid, in the area just in front of the South stone. Allow a little walking space between the fire circle and the stone. Begin the fire by lighting the fire starter log. Carefully use a tiny bit of lighter fluid if needed to help the log catch. Once the log is burning well, add some of the small wood pieces, then a couple of the larger pieces of wood onto the fire. As your fire burns, begin in the West. Light the candle, pour a little of the milk and honey mixture onto each stone and spend a moment in each directional quarter, welcoming that element as you perform this homage. Ending in the South, light the candle, pour the milk and honey mixture onto the south stone, leaving some in the dispenser for later. Sit in front of the fire and feel its warmth. Toss some of the powdered incense into the flames. What colors do you see? Commune with the fire for a few minutes.

Invite fire to join your circle. What do you feel? Close your eyes and feel the heat of the fire on your face and body. Feel it warm and comfort you. Meditate on the blessing that fire is to humans. See it take its many forms of solar heat, electricity, flame. Think of how it cooks our food, purifies our fields and forests for future growth, warms our bodies and our bathing water. Think of all the things that fire in its many forms does for you personally. See our ancestors using wood and coal to keep themselves warm and to cook their food. See them using kerosene lamps for light. Now think of the destruction that fire can bring when it is not treated with respect. Think of electric chairs, huge brush fires, burning homes, nuclear weapons. Think of the way fire can wipe out entire city blocks. See fire burning on an oil slick in the ocean. Learn to respect fire and treat it with care.

Use your power with it, not over it or beneath it. Look into the flames before you. See how they dance with color. Watch the fire burn. Look for visions in the fire. Pay attention to what you see with your third eye while you watch the flames. Think of the flames of passion, both sexual and motivational. Think of something that you really wanted to do with your life and never followed through on. Try to feel the passion you felt for that choice or activity. What is it in your life at this time that you feel a "passion" to accomplish? What burns at you, inside your heart that is your secret desire, your special wish? Meditate on that. What do you want to accomplish more than anything? When you have this firmly in mind, use the lightweight paper and pen and write a request to the fire element that you be shown how to accomplish this in your lifetime and that it be brought to you. Be certain that it is not a request that would bend someone's free will, such as bringing a particular person to you. Next to your signature or sigil at the bottom of the page, apply some of your saliva with your right thumb. Place a little of the saltpeter on the paper and fold into a square. Toss the paper square into the fire and watch it burn. After it has burned away, spend a few more moments with the fire energies.

When you have finished, thank fire for being with you at this ritual. Pinch out the South candle. Go to the remaining directional quarters, extinguishing the candles and thanking the energies. When your circle is lifted, smother the fire with earth. Do not leave the fire burning. Wait fifteen minutes then write about your feelings.

# Water

Water aligns with West and with intuition, emotions, and endings. This exercise should be started with the New Moon and culminate on the Full Moon. You will need:

*One Bottle (Dark or Amber if you have it) with a top or cork*

*Sea Salt, 2 teaspoons*

*A Blue Marble that will fit in the bottle*

*A Bath Tub*

*A stick incense that makes you feel aligned with the element of water, 2-3 sticks*

*Water enough to fill the bottle, then enough to fill the bathtub*

*4 Blue Candles*

*Wooden Matches*

On the night of the New Moon, pour the sea salt into the bottle. Place the marble in the bottle and fill it with water. Place the bottle where it will be in the moon's light until the night of the Full Moon.

On the night of the Full Moon, leave the lights off in the bathroom, light the 4 blue candles and place them where you like in bathroom, preferably around the tub. Light the incense and place in an appropriate holder. Fill tub up with water that is very warm but not extremely hot.

Get into the tub nude, holding the bottle with the salt water and marble inside. Relax in the tub and tune yourself to the element of water. Think about being inside the womb of the Goddess. Think about a time of death and rebirth. Think about all the unwanted obstacles that you want to eliminate in your life. Hold the obstacles firmly in mind and open the bottle. Pour the salt water out into the tub, cleansing yourself to represent the rebirth. Pour the marble into your hand. Ask the energies of water for a gift; something you need or want dearly.

Relax in the tub. Feel the water all around you. Splash the water over your face and body. Think of how water suspends and protects us before we are born. Think of the water from which our ancestors emerged to begin life on dry land. Think of the water that will nourish our grandchildren one day. When finished, step out of the tub, taking your marble with you. Envision that you are leaving the womb of the Goddess. All outmoded aspects of your life that you would like to cast away stay in the tub.

Energy Magic   by Eric & Katrina Rasbold

Take your marble with you to represent your gift. Let the water drain from the tub and things that no longer serve you drain away with it. Thank the element of water for lending energies to your circle. Sleep with the marble in a pouch under your pillow to receive a message in your dreams. The next day, write about your feelings regarding the exercise.

# Chapter 19 - Protection

It would be irresponsible and naïve to write a book about Energy Magic and not include a chapter on protection. We can write about magical ethics all day long and tell you how to keep yourself out of those nasty pitfalls that bring Karma calling in a major way, but there will always be those few who are willing to take the hit in order to harm or manipulate someone else. There may even be those who feel they are well within their rights to launch a magical attack because they have been misinformed or jumped to an inaccurate conclusion about what you have done.

It is highly unlikely that this will ever happen. Usually, when a person feels that they are under magical attack, it is because a series of events has occurred that are disproportionately uncomfortable or negative. After they struggle to find balance, they may feel knocked down by a few occurrences that are even more unfortunate and at that point, it may cross a person's mind that they are under attack. More often what is going on is that they have made some choices that have taken them off of their path to the greatest good and The Universe is self-correcting and attempting to get their attention. The best course of action is to trace back to the last time things were right and do a full autopsy on what has occurred in the interim.

Because of the rarity of actual psychic or magical attack, we do not recommend that you attack back. This puts you in the same set of circumstances of reacting without knowing the full story. There are, however, ways that you can defend yourself without potentially incurring Karmic beatings.

The most effective methods of protection and defense are mirrors and visualization. The first step is to completely cleanse your own energy by body brushing and then smudging.

Sticks of white sage, cedar, sweet grass, lavender, or other cleansing herbs are easily available online or in stores that specialize in Native American items or metaphysical stores. Light the end of the smudge stick and then blow it out so that it smolders.

Pass the smoke over your home and yourself. Take care around the vents, doors, and windows of your home where air passes in and out of the home. If the smudge stick goes a little wild and smoke billows out from it, then you have some negative energy that needs to be dissipated in order to bring cleanliness and balance to your home and environment.

Once you have carried the smoke to all areas of your home, put out the smudge stick by grinding the burning end into a hard, fireproof surface or into sand. Next, use a nicely scented incense to empower the environment and bring positive energy into it again.

When this process is complete and your home is magically cleansed out, use a small mirror of any kind and set it on your altar, in front of your home (it can be hidden and still work) and envision a "reflect and return" process. Imagine that any negativity sent your way is reflected by the mirror and returned to the one who sent it. It never touches you. You can also visualize yourself behind a protective shield or bubble or encased in protective armor.

White light is another strong, protective force. See yourself, your loved ones, and your home enveloped in the purest white light imaginable. Tell yourself that nothing can penetrate the white light unless it is itself "of the light." Negativity may not enter.

We have never seen a case of magical attack or negative energy that we were unable to combat using those methods. Most often, the cause of the "attack" is something the person created themselves, either through misstep or not accepting the messages previously sent by The Universe.

Either way, the exercises of cleansing and protecting will effectively remove any negativity. After that is completed, the person would also be wise to re-evaluate any recent changes or choices that could have thrown their life path off track. Ask The Universe to show you what is out of alignment and how to fix it, then open to the information you receive.

For a full discussion on cleansing your home and personal protection, please see our book *Magical Ethics and Protection*

# Chapter 20 - In Conclusion

We certainly do not claim to have the final word on the nature of God or the particulars of how people approach God. Anyone who makes such a claim is speaking outside of their element, regardless of the degree of education and experience they possess. Any talk of the nature of God, The Universe, etc, is purely speculative and based on what feels right to the person drawing the conclusions.

We recognize and own that many people will be uncomfortable with the content of this book for a number of reasons

*Christians will feel it is too Pagan.*

*Pagans will feel it is too Christianized.*

*Ceremonial and traditional magical people will feel it is too simplified*

*Most people want to believe that their way of engaging God and the natural energies that represent God in our world is the only "right" way.*

*Inclusiveness does not come natural to us as humans. We want to section off into little common cliques and feel special rather than feeling special because of our tremendous degree of similarities.*

*Christians are often uncomfortable with words like "ritual" and "The Universe" or "Goddess."*

*Pagans and Christians alike are often uncomfortable with words like "prayer" and "God" as a genderless form.*

For those who work to overcome those knee jerk reactions, read the rest of the text, and apply the principal, they will find that their relationship to God and the expressions of God inherent through Nature intensifies greatly.

We have walked many spiritual paths, not just through books, but also through actual practice. We now work a blended path called "CUSP: Climbing Up the Spiral Pathway," developed by us in 1997. It puts Energy Magic to use in a very fundamental and continual way, following the ancient agricultural cycles to improve the practitioner's life significantly every single year.

We were both raised as Christians as children and young adults and in that practice, we experienced amazing spiritual moments in the presence of God. Since we left the Christian church, we have encountered God in so many different ways and places. God makes it easy for any of us to have a meaningful spiritual encounter if we do not view Energy Magic or spirituality as a complicated, fearful process. When you work to create a spiritual environment in your everyday life, regardless of your living situation, and engage God on a regular basis, miracles begin to happen seemingly of their own accord. When you add your own "bio" energy to the mix, the process begins to sing and vibrate. It is at that point that you can accomplish almost anything.

In the beginning of this book, the goal we identified to you, the reader, was one of feeling those sacred, spiritual moments on such a regular basis that you truly know that you are living a blessed life; the ordinary life in an extraordinary way. How in the world could the steps we have described to you throughout this book make that happen?

When we effectively eliminate drama in our lives and refuse to entertain its presence at all, we grow closer to God. Drama is loud, demanding, and spiritually devastating.

When we surround ourselves by imagery and visual cues that cause us to feel more spiritually alive and connected, we grow closer to God. As humans, we respond extremely well to visual cues and visual cues tie together what our Conscious Self sees with what our Higher Self feels. It bridges the gap and lets them communicate again.

When we take time to meditate and pray each day, we are making a conscious effort to seek out our Higher Self every day. This not only brings us closer to God but allows us to also know ourselves more intimately.

When we are more proactive with our prayers and communications with God and instill our own working bio energies into the process, we feel more connected to God and more involved with the process of manifesting our own greatest good.

Soon, with concerted practice, every moment begins to feel sacred and we feel plugged into the pulse of The Universe in a profound way. Once you have lived life in this fashion, it feels cheap and dull to go back to "the way things were." It is as though your eyes open and you see layers to your choices and experiences that were not there before. Because your thoughts, words, and actions take on a greater significance, you begin to use them more carefully and deliberately. Energy Magic changes who you are in the world in a particularly rewarding and meaningful way.

Divine guidance comes to you more easily and is more readily apparent. When you are faced with a choice, one path will "light up" more than another will and you will be able to sense what should be done faster than before.

You will take on a more significant relationship with earth, air, fire, and water as you see them as extensions of God's hand in the world. You will begin to see the intricate nature of The Universe and how all choices and experiences interconnect to create that grand concert of magic; the concert that was in place long before you were born and that will continue long afterward.

It is a pleasure and an honor to bring this process to you. It is by no means a new system. Christians, Pagans, and other religions have done it for thousands of years. It is simply about stripping away the politics, the drama, the fearfulness, and the convoluted practice and getting down to a very simple means of connecting with the Divine and creating a blessed and sacred life here on earth.

# APPENDIX 1 – Magical Color Correspondences

The following colors are the most commonly used colors in Energy Magic. You can use the power of colors in many ways, including the items you use in your ritual, the clothing you wear, and the candles you burn outside of ritual.

**White** – Spirituality, cleansing, purity, perfection, innocence, integrity, healing, freedom, opportunity, forgiveness, and acceptance. It is also a color of simple power. White may be used to substitute for any other color. Because it reflects and radiates, white will also enhance the power of other color magic in spell work. It eliminates negative energy and creates inner peace. It also corresponds to the Maiden aspect of the Goddess archetypes.

**Black** – Death, the Underworld, grounding, stability, mystery and magic. Absorbs negative energy and is good for minimizing a particular energy (pulling back a spell you want to erase, for instance). Rather than the absence of color, black is the presence of all colors so, like white, it may be used as a substitute for any other color. Whereas white is projective, black absorbs. Black corresponds to the Crone aspect of the Goddess archetypes.

**Red** – Element of Fire, the Root Chakra, the God Ares, Mars, love, passion, sex, self-confidence, success, strength, creativity, persistence, energy, and vitality. Good for love and healing spells, associated with the Root Chakra and with any powerful emotion. Red corresponds to the Mother aspect of the Goddess archetypes.

**Pink** – Love from the heart, nurturing, tenderness, sensitivity, harmony, femininity and innocence. While red is associated with fiery love and passion, pink corresponds to the gentler aspects of these emotions. Pink is also good for spell work involving new skin growth and regeneration.

**Orange** – The Sacral (Navel) Chakra, harvest time, happiness, excitement, assertiveness, motivation, persistence, and prosperity. Great for eliminating procrastination, anxiety, and stress. It is also helpful when trying to divine solutions or new ways of accomplishing your goals.

**Yellow** – The Solar Plexus Chakra, the Sun and Sun God(s), joy, cheerfulness, intellect, hope, direction, personal power, clear thinking, concentration, fruitfulness, and communication. Great for banishing fear and treachery. This is particularly true for bright yellows.

**Green** – The Heart Chakra, the Earth Goddess, the Element Earth, the Green Man (or Horned God), nature, wealth, abundance, longevity, and healing. Used in color magic spells for healing, grounding, establishing stability and for drawing wealth and prosperity to you.

Energy Magic   by Eric & Katrina Rasbold

**Blue** – The Throat Chakra, the Element Water, communication, creativity, integrity, calmness, truth, loyalty, justice, leadership and clear thinking. It is said that a lie cannot be maintained while a blue candle burns. Blue "balances the scales" and equalizes debts.

**Indigo** - The Brow (or Pineal, or Third Eye) Chakra, idealism, justice, wisdom, inspiration, intuition, spirituality, psychic powers and the understanding of things. It can also be used in color magic to help reduce phobias and stress, as well as seeking out one's higher self and connectivity to Deity and other benevolent energies.

**Violet or Purple** - The Crown Chakra, inspiration, spirituality, the sacred, selflessness, tolerance, intuition, imagination, royalty, wealth, inner peace, security, protection, creativity, freedom, and personal responsibility. It is used in spells for protection and psychic ability and for results that are "the highest and the best."

**Brown** – Grounding, good health, hard work, stability, reward from effort, and element of Earth. Like white, it has the power to enhance other colors in color magic.

**Gold** – The Sun, masculine energy, success, money, abundance, power, positivity, confidence, self-motivation, self-discipline, generosity, enlightenment, and manifestation. The color is very useful is spells for success, wealth, and self-confidence. Note that Fool's Gold (Iron Pyrite) has this power (despite of the negativity of the name) and is frequently used for drawing wealth.

**Silver** – The Moon, feminine energy, balance, harmony, change, learning, introspection, confidence, wealth, secrets, hidden desires and intuition. It is very useful in divination and meditation. It is also useful for tapping into and increasing your psychic power and/or intuition. On occasion, silver is used for money drawing spells.

**Grey** – Used to work through morning, sorrow, humility, doubt, and uncertainty. It is also good for obscuring what you do not want to have seen "a gray area" and creating confusion.

# APPENDIX 2 – Magical Scent Correspondences

Listed below are common scents used in incenses, powdered, stick, and cone, in potpourri, and in blended oils, along with their properties. Most will mention several properties. The purpose that will be amplified is the one that is in keeping with the energy you generate toward you goal.

**Allspice:** Money, Luck, Healing.

**Apple:** Love, Healing, Garden Magic, Immortality. Apples can be used for poppets or the apple wood carved into a poppet.

**Basil:** Love, Exorcism, Wealth, Protection. Causes sympathy between two people and soothes tempers between lovers. Courage.

**Bergamot, Orange:** Money.

**Blueberry:** Protection.

**Cedar:** Healing, Purification, Money, Protection.

**Chamomile:** Money, Sleep, Love, Purification.

**Cherry:** Love, Divination.

**Cinnamon:** Spirituality, Success, Healing, Power, Psychic Powers, Lust, Protection, Love. Aids in healing. Draws money. Stimulates psychic power and produces protective vibrations. Great in sachets and amulets.

**Clove:** Protection, Exorcism, Love, Money. Worn or carried, they attract the opposite sex.

**Coconut:** Purification, Protection, Chastity

**Copal:** Love, Purification.

**Daffodil:** Love, Fertility, Luck

**Dragon's Blood:** Love, Protection, Exorcism, Potency. A powerful protectant when sprinkled around the house or burned as incense. A pinch added to other incenses will increase their potency.

**Eucalyptus:** Healing, Protection

**Frankincense:** Protection, Exorcism, Spirituality.

**Ginger:** Love, Money, Success, Power

**Grape:** Fertility, Garden Magic, Mental Powers, Money

**Hemp:** Healing, Love, Vision, Meditation

**Honeysuckle:** Money, Psychic Powers, Protection. Increases spiritual connections. It enhances understanding of images and impressions collected in the astral.

**Jasmine:** Love, Money, Prophetic Dreams

**Lavender:** Love, Protection, Sleep, Chastity (with rosemary), Longevity, Purification, Happiness, Peace

**Lemon:** Longevity, Purification, Love, Friendship

**Lemon Balm:** Love. Success. Healing, especially for those with mental or nervous disorders. Gives energy to make one more desirable to the opposite sex.

**Lemongrass:** Repel Snakes, Lust, Psychic Powers

**Lemon Verbena:** Purification, Love

**Lilac:** Exorcism, Protection

**Lime:** Healing, Love, Protection

**Mint:** Money, Love, Lust, Healing, Exorcism, Travel, Protection

**Myrrh:** Protection, Exorcism, Healing, Spirituality

**Orange:** Love, Divination, Luck, Money

**Patchouli:** Money, Fertility, Lust

**Peach:** Love, Exorcism, Longevity, Fertility, Wishes

**Pear:** Lust, Love

**Peppermint:** Purification, Sleep, Love, Healing, Psychic Powers

**Pine:** Healing, Fertility, Protection, Exorcism, Money

**Pineapple:** Luck, Money, Chastity

**Pomegranate:** Divination, Luck, Wishes, Wealth, Fertility

**Raspberry:** Protection, Love

**Rose:** Love, Psychic Powers, Healing, Love, Divination, Luck, Protection

**Rosemary:** Protection, Love, Lust, Mental Powers, Exorcism, Purification, Healing, Sleep, Youth

**Sage:** Immortality, Longevity, Wisdom, Protection, Wishes, Cleansing and Purifying, Dispelling negativity.

**Sandalwood:** Protection, Healing, Exorcism, Spirituality

**Spearmint:** Healing, Love, Mental Powers

**Strawberry:** Love, Luck

**Sunflower:** Fertility, Wishes, Health, Wisdom

**Sweetgrass:** Calling Spirits, Cleansing and Purifying, Blessings

**Sweetpea:** Friendship, Chastity, Courage, Strength

**Thyme:** Health, Healing, Sleep, Psychic Powers, Love, Purification, Courage

**Tobacco:** Healing, Purification

**Vanilla:** Love, Lust, Mental Powers

**Violet:** Protection, Love, Lust, Luck, Wishes, Peace, Healing

**Wintergreen:** Protection

# APPENDIX 3 – Magical Herb Properties

Herbs may be used in many ways for Energy Magic purposes. The most common are burning (to release the energy inside) or sprinkling into focus bags. It is essential that you thoroughly research an herb before you use it to check for toxicity and other potential dangers. Those listed below are easily obtainable through internet sources or locally in herb shops, health food stores, or metaphysical shops.

**African Violet:** Spirituality, Protection. Promotes spirituality when grown in the home.

**Alfalfa:** Prosperity, Anti-hunger, Money. Brings in money and protects against financial misfortune.

**Allspice:** Money, Luck, Healing.

**Almond:** Money, Prosperity, Wisdom.

**Aloe:** Protection, Luck. Guards against evil influences and prevents household accidents. Prevents feelings of loneliness.

**Angelica:** Exorcism, Protection, Healing, Visions. Angelica protects in two ways: it creates a barrier against negative energy and fills you with good, radiant energy. Great for use in "reflect and return" magic. Enhances the aura. Gives a joyful outlook on life.

**Anise Seed:** Protection. Purification. Youth. Deals with inner, personal issues related to lack of fulfillment. Helps one to become more open to happiness and enjoy company of others. Repels nightmares. Brings protection when traveling in the astral. It is the essential taste in licorice.

**Apple:** Love, Healing, Garden Magic, Immortality.

**Ash:** Protection, Prosperity, Sea Rituals, Health. An ash staff wards off evil. Healing wands should be made of ash wood. Burning ash at Yule brings prosperity. Carry the leaves to gain love.

**Aspen:** Eloquence, Anti-Theft.

**Aster:** Use in love sachets, or carry the bloom to win love.

**Bachelor's Buttons:** Love. Women wear this flower on their breast to attract love.

**Balm of Gilead:** Love, Manifestations, Protection, Healing. Carry the buds to mend a broken heart.

**Bamboo:** Protection, Luck, Hex-Breaking, Wishes.

**Barley:** Love, Healing, Protection. Use the grain or barley water in love spells.

**Basil:** Love, Exorcism, Wealth, Protection. Causes sympathy between two people and soothes tempers between lovers. Courage.

**Bay (Laurel):** Protection, Psychic Powers, Healing, Purification, Strength. Used in clairvoyance and wisdom brews. Place leaves under pillow for prophetic dreams. Burn to cause vision. Attracts love and romance. Bay leaves impart strength to athletes.

**Beech:** To have wishes granted.

**Birch:** Protection, Exorcism, Purification.

**Black Cohosh:** Love, Courage, Protection, Potency, Purging

**Blackberry:** Healing, Money, Protection.

**Bladderwrack:** Protection, Sea Spells, Wind Spells, Money, Psychic Powers

**Bloodroot:** TOXIC!! Love, Protection, Purification.

**Boneset:** Protection. Exorcism.

**Broom:** TOXIC! Purification, Protection, Wind work, Divination. Blooms bring good fortune and plenty.

**Buckthorn:** Protection, Exorcism, Wishes, Legal Matters. Mixing Buckthorn into the herbs for any magical work will bind the herb powers together and amplify their energy.

**Camellia:** Brings riches and luxury.

**Caraway:** Protection, Lust, Health, Anti-Theft, Mental Powers, aids memory

**Cardamom:** Lust, Love.

**Carnation:** Protection, Strength, Healing.

**Cascara Sagrada:** Legal Matters, Money, Protection. Sprinkle infusion around your home before going to court. It will help you win your case.

**Catnip:** Cat Magic, Love, Beauty, Happiness. Attracts good spirits and great luck. Used in beauty and happiness spells.

**Cedar:** Healing, Purification, Money, Protection. The smoke is purifying and chases away bad dreams

**Chamomile:** Money, Sleep, Love, Purification. Sprinkle around property to remove curses and spells cast against you.

**Chicory:** Removing Obstacles, Encouraging Frugality. Carry to remove all obstacles that might crop up in your life.

**Chili Pepper:** Fidelity, Love.

**Chrysanthemum:** Protection. Promotes mental health.

**Cinnamon:** Spirituality, Success, Healing, Power, Psychic Powers, Lust, Protection, Love. Draws money. Stimulates psychic power and produces protective vibrations.

**Cinquefoil:** The five points of the leaves represent love, money, health, power, and wisdom. If carried, all these will be granted. Good for love magic and to promote an abundant harvest. Contains energy dedicated to bringing your goals into fruition.

**Clove:** Protection, Exorcism, Love, Money. Worn or carried, they attract the opposite sex.

**Clover:** Protection, Love, Money, Fidelity, Exorcism, Success.

**Coconut:** Purification, Protection, Chastity

**Comfrey:** Good for any magical healing. Worn or carried, it ensures safety during travel. The root is used in money spells.

**Copal:** Love, Purification.

**Coriander:** Love, Health, Healing.

**Cumin:** Protection, Fidelity, Exorcism, Anti-theft. Burned with frankincense for protection and scattered on the floor (sometimes with salt) to drive out evil. When given to a lover, promotes fidelity.

**Daffodil:** Love, Fertility, Luck

**Daisy:** Lust, Luck

**Damiana:** Lust, Love, Visions

**Dandelion:** Divination, Wishes, Calling Spirits

**Dill:** Protection, Money, Lust, Luck

**Dogwood:** Wishes, Protection.

**Dragon's Blood:** Love, Protection, Exorcism, Potency. A powerful protectant when sprinkled around the house or burned as incense. A pinch added to to other incenses will increase their potency.

**Echinacea:** Strength, Healing

**Elecampane:** Love, Protection, Psychic Powers

**Eucalyptus:** Healing, Protection

**Eyebright:** Mental Powers, Psychic Powers

**Fennel:** Protection, Healing, Purification

**Fenugreek:** Money

**Fern:** Rain Making, Protection, Luck, Riches, Health, Exorcism

**Feverfew:** Protection

**Flax:** Money, Protection, Beauty, Psychic Powers, Healing

**Frankincense:** Protection, Exorcism, Spirituality. Frankincense is considered to be one of the "Temple Incenses" that is used to consecrate and bless a sacred space.

**Gardenia:** Love, Peace, Healing, Spirituality

**Garlic:** Protection, Healing, Exorcism, Lust, Anti-Theft

**Geranium:** Fertility, Love, Health, Protection

**Ginger:** Love, Money, Success, Power

**Ginseng:** Love, Wishes, Healing, Beauty, Protection, Lust

**Goldenrod:** Money, Divination

**Goldenseal:** Healing, Money, Purging

**Grape:** Fertility, Garden Magic, Mental Powers, Money

**Hawthorn:** Fertility, Chastity, Fishing Magic, Happiness

**Hazel:** Luck, Fertility, Anti-Lightning, Protection, Wishes

**Heather:** Protection, Rain Making, Luck.

**Heliotrope:** Exorcism, Prophetic Dreams, Healing, Wealth, Invisibility

**Hemp:** Healing, Love, Vision, Meditation

**Hibiscus:** Lust, Love, Divination

**High John the Conqueror:** Money, Love, Success, Happiness

**Holly:** Protection, Luck, Dream Magic.

**Honeysuckle:** Money, Psychic Powers, Protection.

**Hops:** Healing, Sleep

**Horehound:** Protection, Mental Powers, Exorcism, Healing

**Hyacinth:** Love, Protection, Happiness

**Hyssop:** Purification, Protection

**Iris:** Purification, Wisdom

**Jasmine:** Love, Money, Prophetic Dreams

**Jobs Tears:** Healing, Wishes, Luck

**Juniper:** Protection, Anti-Theft, Love, Exorcism, Health

**Kava-Kava:** Visions, Protection, Luck

**Knotweed:** Binding, Health

**Lady's Slipper:** Protection

**Lavender:** Love, Protection, Sleep, Chastity (with rosemary), Longevity, Purification, Happiness, Peace

**Lemon:** Longevity, Purification, Love, Friendship

**Lemon Balm:** Love. Success. Healing, especially for those with mental or nervous disorders.

**Lemongrass:** Lust, Psychic Powers

**Lemon Verbena:** Purification, Love

**Lilac:** Exorcism, Protection

**Lily:** Protection, Breaking Love Spells

**Lily of the Valley:** Mental Powers, Happiness

**Lovage:** Love

**Lucky Hand:** Employment, Powerful Luck Magic, Protection, Money, Travel

**Magnolia:** Fidelity

**Maidenhair:** Beauty, Love

**Male Fern:** Luck, Love

**Marigold (Calendula):** Protection, Prophetic Dreams, Legal Matters, Psychic Powers. Carry marigold petals with a bay leaf to quiet gossip.

**Marjoram:** Protection, Love, Happiness, Health, Money

**Meadowsweet:** Love, Divination, Peace, Happiness

**Mint:** Money, Love, Lust, Healing, Exorcism, Travel, Protection

**Mistletoe:** Protection, Love, Hunting, Fertility, Health, Exorcism.

**Mugwort:** Strength, Psychic Powers, Protection, Prophetic Dreams, Healing, Astral Projection. Carried, it also increases lust and fertility.

**Mullein:** Courage, Protection, Health, Love, Divination, Exorcism

**Mustard:** Fertility, Protection, Mental Powers

**Myrrh:** Protection, Exorcism, Healing, Spirituality

**Myrtle:** Love, Fertility, Youth, Peace, Money

**Nettle:** "Sister Nettle" A powerful herb that is good for Exorcism, Protection, Healing and Lust

**Oak:** Protection, Health, Money, Healing, Potency, Fertility, Luck

**Orange:** Love, Divination, Luck, Money

**Orange Bergamot:** Money. Put leaves in wallet or purse to attract money. Rub fresh leaves on money before spending

**Parsley:** Love, Protection, Purification

**Passion Flower:** Peace, Sleep, Friendship

**Patchouli:** Money, Fertility, Lust

**Pennyroyal:** Strength, Protection, Peace, Cleansing and Purging

Energy Magic   by Eric & Katrina Rasbold

**Peppermint:** Purification, Sleep, Love, Healing, Psychic Powers

**Periwinkle:** TOXIC!! Love, Lust, Mental Powers, Money, Protection. Banishes negative energy. Makes one feel desirable.

**Pine:** Healing, Fertility, Protection, Exorcism, Money

**Poke:** Courage, Repels Negativity

**Poppy:** Fertility, Love, Sleep, Money, Luck,

**Primrose:** Protection, Love

**Ragweed:** Courage

**Rose:** Love, Psychic Powers, Healing, Love, Divination, Luck, Protection

**Rosemary:** Protection, Love, Lust, Mental Powers, Exorcism, Purification, Healing, Sleep, Youth

**Rue:** Healing, Health, Mental Powers, Exorcism, Love

**Saffron:** Love, Healing, Happiness, Wind Raising, Lust, Strength, Psychic Powers, Wealth & Prosperity

**Sage:** Immortality, Longevity, Wisdom, Protection, Wishes, Cleansing and Purifying, Dispelling negativity.

**Sagebrush:** Purification, Exorcism

**St. John's Wort:** Health, Power, Protection, Strength, Love, Divination, Happiness

**Sandalwood:** Protection, Healing, Exorcism, Spirituality

**Sassafras:** Health, Money

**Skullcap:** Love, Fidelity, Peace

**Slippery Elm:** Halts Gossip

**Snapdragon:** Protection

**Solomon's Seal:** Protection, Exorcism

**Sorrel Wood:** Healing, Health

**Spanish Moss:** Protection

**Spearmint:** Healing, Love, Mental Powers

**Spikenard:** Love

**Star Anise:** Psychic Powers, Luck

**Sunflower:** Fertility, Wishes, Health, Wisdom

**Sweetgrass:** Calling Spirits, Cleansing and Purifying, Blessings

**Sweetpea:** Friendship, Chastity, Courage, Strength

**Tansy:** Health, Longevity

**Thistle:** Strength, Protection, Repelling Negativity, Healing

**Thyme:** Health, Healing, Sleep, Psychic Powers, Love, Purification, Courage

**Tobacco:** Healing, Purification

**Tonka Bean: TOXIC!!!** Love. Money. Courage. Wishes. Used extensively in love sachets and mixtures, and carried to attract love. Also worn or carried to attract money, bring luck, grant courage, and ward off illness.

**Turmeric:** Purification

**Uva Ursa:** Psychic Workings

**Valerian:** Love, Sleep, Purification, Protection

**Vanilla:** Love, Lust, Mental Powers

**Vervain:** Love, Protection, Purification, Peace, Money, Healing. Protects the wearer from negative emotions and depression. Instills a love of learning.

**Vetivert:** Love, Repels Negativity, Luck, Money, Anti-Theft

**Violet:** Protection, Love, Lust, Luck, Wishes, Peace, Healing

**Wheat:** Fertility, Money

**Willow:** Love, Divination, Protection, Healing

**Wintergreen:** Protection, Healing, Repels Negativity

**Witch Hazel:** Protection, Chastity

**Woodruff:** Victory, Protection, Money

**Wormwood:** Psychic Powers, Protection, Love, Calling Spirits

**Yarrow:** Courage, Love, Psychic Powers, Exorcism

**Yerba Mate:** Fidelity, Love, Lust

**Yucca:** Transmutation, Protection, Purification.

# APPENDIX 4 – Poppet Pattern

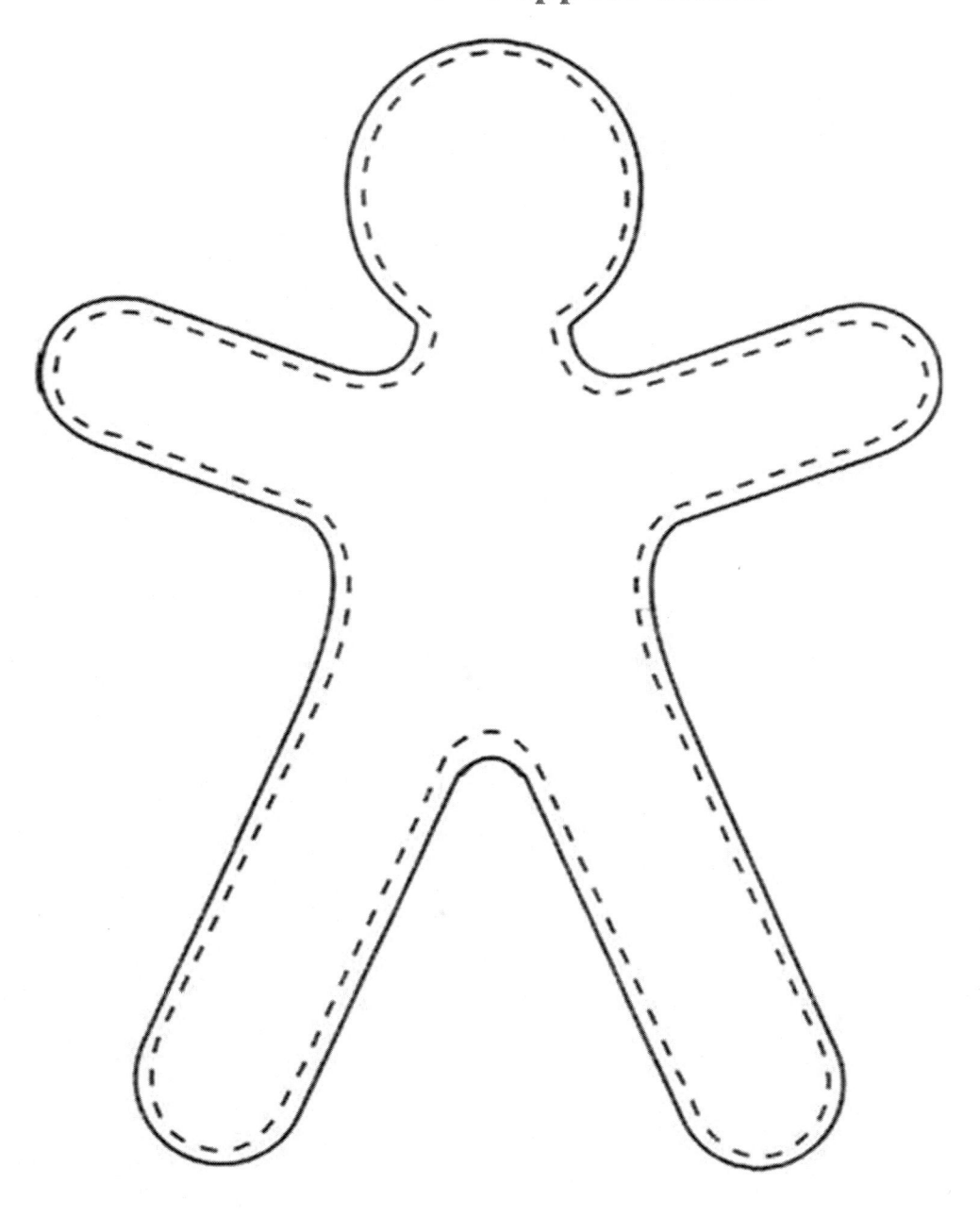

Energy Magic   by Eric & Katrina Rasbold

# APPENDIX 5 – Magical Properties of Stones

Listed below are some of the more common stones used for their magical energy. Stones may be worn in jewelry or focus bags, carried in pockets, or placed on your altar or other sacred space.

**Agate** – Known for its intricate patterns of color, mostly dark brown and deep red. It promotes protection, victory, love, fertility in crops, fidelity, energy boosts, promoting intelligence and mental agility, turning away evil spirits, curing insomnia, and pleasant dreams. Agate is great for chakra clearing and removing energy blockages that can cause illness.

**Moss Agate** - Dark green in color, this stone promotes eloquence and persuasion, fertility, eternal life, healing, psychic powers, scrying, astral travel, contacting spirit guides, wealth, happiness, long life, and friendship.

**Amber** – This looks like a deep orange or yellow stone, but is actually fossilized tree sap. It is frequently used at the base of wands.

**Amethyst** – This beautiful purple stone is a type of quartz and is known to be a strong healing crystal. It is good or all physical, mental, and emotional disorders. It purifies the blood and balances the chakras. It is also good for clairvoyance and the ability to see through illusion. Amethyst crystals are often found on the projecting end of wands.

**Aventurine** - A dark green type of quartz, sometimes called Indian Jade, this lucky stone is used to release anxieties and bring about good attitudes, vibrant health, and independence. Strongly connected to the elemental of Earth, it has balancing and calming energy. It is protective and can enhance visualization and all forms of the arts. It attracts prosperity, love, and adventures.

**Bloodstone** – This is a deep green stone with red flecks or stripes through it like blood. It is a form of chalcedony. It is also called Heliotrope. It is connected to the root and heart chakras and stimulates the kundalini life force. It protects against deception and helps preserve health and create prosperity. It is also good for self-confidence and can purify the blood, remove toxins, heal friendships or draw in love.

**Calcite** – This somewhat soft stone can be found in green, pink, blue, golden brown and many other colors. It is often used in marble architecture. It helps clear negative influences from the environment, purifies the body, and attracts love. It's very calming.

**Carnelian** - This vibrant orange or read stone is traditionally used to guard against negative energy sent toward the wearer. It speeds up all manifestations, and increases the sense of self-worth. It is good for career changes and overall success and supports organizational abilities.

**Citrine** – This is a very clear, yellow type of quartz that, like most quartz, is often used in wand making. It helps maintain connect with Higher Self and increases clarity of thought. It can increase creative energy and is good for attracting prosperity and abundance.

**Hematite** – This is shiny, dark gray stone that is red when powdered. It is good for winning court cases and is a protector of valiant warriors. It energizes and purifies the blood and boosts optimism, will power and courage.

**Jade** – Most people are familiar with the beautiful oriental green jade, but it can also be white, pink, yellow, black, gray, or brown. Jade strengthens the heart, kidneys, lymphatic system, and immune system. It increases fertility, balances the emotions, dispels negativity, and develops courage and wisdom. Green jade in particular is known to grant vivid and prophetic dreams.

**Jasper** – Jasper is actually a type of chalcedony that is most often reddish in color, but may actually come in a variety of colors. Bloodstone is a type of jasper. Jasper is good for changing the weather, healing stomach problems, balancing the chakras and balancing energy. It can dispel nightmares and is very grounding and stabilizes the emotions well.

**Lapis Lazuli** – This beautiful blue variegated stone is actually a combination of several minerals and is associated with the throat chakra. It heals the astral body and is a very fortunate stone to carry. It can ease tension and anxiety, increase mental clarity and help overcome depression.

**Malachite** – This protective dark green stone often has streaks of lighter great running through it. It strengthens intuitive powers and is good for "wind walking" or spirit travel. Legend says it will break in half to warn the wearer of impending danger (I have actually seen this happen). It is good for revitalizing the mind, body, and spirit connecting and bringing the three into balance.

**Moonstone** – This beautiful opalescent stone is famous for its milky, otherworldly appearance. It may be opaque white or also have pinkish tones to it. It is excellent for bringing about new beginnings and is a wonderful stone for granting very personal wishes and bringing to you exactly what you need.

**Onyx** – Onyx is a deep black stone that is excellent for absorbing all negative energies and rendering them harmless. It is good for balancing male and female attributes and assist in managing challenging life changes

**Quartz Crystal** – Truly one of the most versatile and magical stones, this is the most commonly used product for wand making, scrying ("crystal" balls) and amplifying your magical energy. This stone is excellent for healing (amethyst and clear quartz are often place over the body at the point where the illness is centered) as well as amplifying psychic abilities and visualization.

**Rose Quartz** - Rose quartz is great for boosting self-esteem and learning to love yourself. It reduces stress and anxiety. It is associated with the crown chakra and as such, boosts connection to the sacred influences in life. It is wonderful for healing old wounds that still impact your life.

**Smoky Quartz** – This beautiful grayish quartz which is great for grounding and centering up. It is effective at blocking negativity and is associated with the root chakra of security.

**Rutilated Quartz** – This quartz is a clear quartz with veins of gold or titanium running through it. This amplifies the power of the quartz and increases the kundalini life force. It grounds negative energy before it impacts the wearer and increases all forms of magical effort. This stone is the 2:1 stone because it is said to double the impact of all magical energy you send out.

**Tourmaline** – This powerful stone is tremendously adept at grounding and centering. It reduces fear and assists the wearer in "walking between the world" and participating in Shaman journeys to "the other side." It is used to form a gateway between the two worlds.

**Rhodonite** – This is a beautiful stone that looks like a patchwork of pink/rose color and gray or black. It is an excellent stress reliever and effectively calms the mind. It balances energy levels and is associated with the heart chakra, so it also brings relationships into balance. It is also said in increase attention to fine details.

**Tiger's-Eye** – This beautiful black, golden brown, and/or yellow stone is a type of chalcedony. It is a "love it or hate it" stone because it carries with it a strong energy of independence. People who fear being on their own or establishing independence often are uncomfortable with the stone. It balances the emotions and gives clear insight into a situation. It is great for discerning the truth in a situation.

**Turquoise** – This sky blue or greenish-blue stone is a powerful tool for drawing in rain and providing protection and prosperity to the wearer. It is said that one should never buy Turquoise for oneself and that it should always be a gift from another. It is excellent for astral travel and a tremendous aid in communication.

## About the Authors

Eric and Katrina Rasbold are the co-founders of CUSP and have worked to develop the path and teaching its principles to students since 1997. They are happily married and live in the remote mountain community of Grizzly Flats, California where they enjoy a rural, blessed lifestyle. They have six children, ranging in age from teens to 40s.

Both Eric and Katrina are avid students of human spirituality and have devoted their entire adult lives to the exploration of the many ways human beings connect to God and vice versa.

Eric and Katrina own and operate Two Sisters Botánica, previously located in Roseville, California, but now solely an online enterprise. You can find their magical products at www.twosistersbotanica.com. They are featured speakers at festivals throughout California, including Pantheacon in San Jose, California. Katrina and Eric's online classes are available at no charge at www.gringabruja.com.

## More Books by the Authors

How to Be a Queen

Beyond Energy Magic *

CUSP: A New Way to Walk An Old Path *

Properties of Magical Energy *

Reuniting the Two Selves *

Magical Ethics and Protection *

The Art of Ritual Crafting *

The Magic and Making of Candles and Soaps

Days and Times of Power *

Crossing the Third Threshold *

How to Create a Magical Working Group

An Insider's Guide to the General Hospital Fan Club Weekend

Leaving Kentucky in the Broad Daylight

The Real Magic *

Get Your Book Published

Goddess in the Kitchen: The Magic and Making of Food

Spiritual Childbirth

Tarot For Real People

Weather or Not

Weather Witchery

Where the Daffodils Grow **

The Daughters of Avalon **

Rose of Avalon **

Aster of Avalon **

Iris of Avalon **

The Dance Card **

* Part of the Bio-Universal Energy Series

** Fiction

Made in United States
North Haven, CT
28 May 2024